THE ISLE OF MAN

By the same author

I RETURN TO SCOTLAND
I RETURN TO SWITZERLAND
I RETURN TO IRELAND
I RETURN TO WALES
THE LAND OF THE CINQUE PORTS
LITTLE ENGLAND BEYOND WALES
THE RIVIERA—NEW LOOK AND OLD
ARDEN AND AVON
NORWEGIAN ODYSSEY
THE CHANNEL ISLANDS

and numerous other works

First published 1954

SET IN 12 ON 13 PT. GARAMOND, AND PRINTED
AND MADE IN GREAT BRITAIN BY PAGE BROS. (NORWICH) LTD.
FOR CHRISTOPHER JOHNSON PUBLISHERS LTD.,
11/14 STANHOPE MEWS WEST, LONDON, S.W.7

Bradda Head, Port Erin

S. P. B. MAIS

THE
ISLE
OF
MAN

WITH 15 PLATES
AND ONE MAP

CHRISTOPHER JOHNSON

LONDON

For
JILL,
LALAGE
and
IMOGEN
with all my love.

CONTENTS

TUESDAY   We Arrive   p. 9

WEDNESDAY   Hall Caine's House—Tynwald Hill—Peel—Laxey—Ramsey   12

THURSDAY   Douglas — The Museum — Bathing Beauty Competition   23

FRIDAY   The House of Keys—Castle Rushen—Castletown — Port St. Mary — Cregneish—The Calf of Man   31

SATURDAY   The Curragh—Sulby Glen—Onchan — Niarbyl — Dalby — Glen Maye   63

SUNDAY   Kirk Braddan—Maughold   77

MONDAY   Port Erin   83

TUESDAY   Garwick Glen — Ramsey — Bride—Jurby   88

WEDNESDAY   Peel—Sheep Dog Trials, Quarter Bridge—The T.T. Course   99

THURSDAY   A Wet Day   110

FRIDAY   Snaefell—The Aquarium, Port Erin   113

SATURDAY   A Walk to Port Soderick   116

SUNDAY   Port St. Mary   119

MONDAY   King William's College — Rushen Abbey   122

TUESDAY   The National Museum—The Experimental Farm, Patrick—Bishop's Court—Glen Helen   128

WEDNESDAY   The Nunnery—St. John's Cattle Mart—Foxdale Mines   137

THURSDAY   We Depart   151

List of Illustrations

Bradda Head, Port Erin	*frontispiece*
The Harbour, Douglas	*facing p.* 14
Country Road near St. John's	15
Elphin Glen with view of Ramsey	48
Guthrie's Memorial, T.T. Course, near Ramsey	49
Port Erin	64
Port St. Mary	65
The Chasms, with the Sugar Loaf Rock	80
A Cottage in Cregneish	81
Injebreck Valley	96
Ballaglass Glen	97
Castle Rushen, Castletown	112
Peel Castle	113
Niarbyl	128
Laxey Wheel	129

I am indebted to the Isle of Man Tourist Board for permission to reproduce these illustrations and for unfailing help and courtesies extended in other respects.

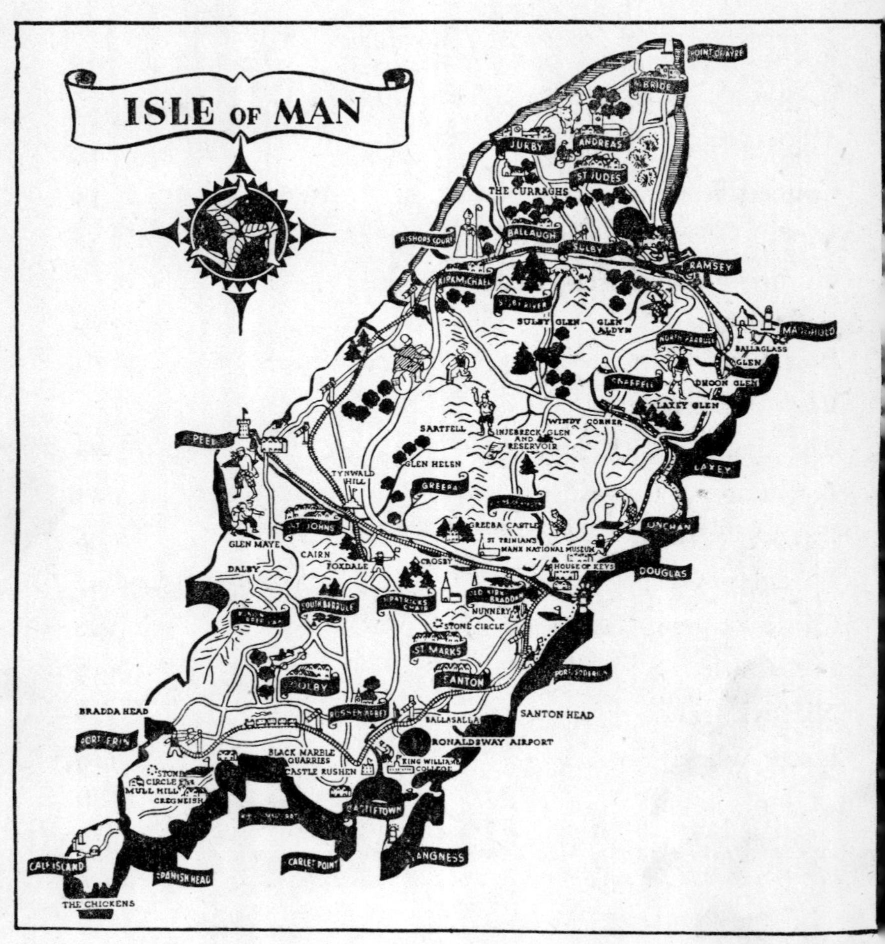

ISLE of MAN
POINT OF AYRE
BRIDE
JURBY
ANDREAS
ST JUDES
THE CURRAGHS
BISHOPS COURT
BALLAUGH
SULBY
RAMSEY
KIRKMICHAEL
SULBY RIVER
SULBY GLEN
GLEN ALDYN
NORTH BARRULE
MAUGHOLD
BALLAGLASS GLEN
CHRE FELL
DHOON GLEN
LAXEY GLEN
SARTFELL
INJEBRECK GLEN AND RESERVOIR
WINDY CORNER
PEEL
GLEN HELEN
LAXEY
TYNWALD HILL
GREEBA
ONCHAN
ST JOHNS
GREEBA CASTLE
ST TRINIANS
MANX NATIONAL MUSEUM
GLEN MAYE
CAIRN
CROSBY
HOUSE OF KEYS
DOUGLAS
DALBY
FOXDALE
OLD KIRK BRADDAN
SOUTH BARRULE
ST PATRICKS CHAIR
NUNNERY
STONE CIRCLE
ST MARKS
COLBY
SANTON
PORT SODERICK
BRADDA HEAD
RUSHEN ABBEY
BALLASALLA
SANTON HEAD
PORT ERIN
BLACK MARBLE QUARRIES
RONALDSWAY AIRPORT
KING WILLIAM COLLEGE
STONE CIRCLE
MULL HILL
CREGNEISH
CASTLE RUSHEN
CASTLETOWN
CALF ISLAND
SPANISH HEAD
CARLE POINT
LANGNESS
THE CHICKENS

In a high north-west wind and a choppy sea we crossed
to the Isle of Man on the afternoon of Tuesday, 7th July.
We had arrived at Liverpool at 11.40 from Birmingham,
but on driving with our baggage to the red and black
funnelled ship *King Orry*, we were told that we couldn't
go on board till 2.30, so we drove back to the Adelphi
Hotel which was crowded with Canadians about to sail in
the very handsome, white, *Empress of Scotland* that was
berthed alongside the *King Orry*.

It was a wild day, a very wild day for July. I drank
several whiskies and ginger ales before sailing as I always
do for setting out on a voyage, even across the Channel.
I haven't the faintest idea whether that is a real preventive of
sea sickness.   Or do I just imagine it ?

I also, to Jill's disgust, took Kwells, though I am never
ill and she always feels that she is going to be. This time
I induced her to take a pill too.

We had a filling luncheon which cost 8s. 6d. each.   All
the tables were taken either by groups of youngish business
men or rather fat and tough-looking Canadians. Liverpool
looked emptier than usual but wore as prosperous a look
as Birmingham.   Money is obviously coming back.

We got down to the ship at 2.45 and to our surprise
found that we had it almost to ourselves. In spite of the
high wind which whistled through the rigging ominously,
and the drenching showers, a solitary girl stood on the
top deck in a bare-backed sun suit.   There were a few small
boys, a number of elderly men and women whose Lancastrian accent betrayed a complete triumph over the Ministry of Education's efforts to impose the effete accents of
the South on the resilient North.

I was introduced to the Manx Captain who was bothered by the proximity of the *Empress of Scotland*, and to the steward who told me that he had one private cabin left which we could use if we wanted it. We decided to stay in the lounge where there was plenty of room. There was less room on the upper deck which I paced till the driving rain drove me in.

I watched with considerable interest the sea getting rougher as we safely turned, tug-drawn, away from the huge Canadian liner, down the winding channel of the Mersey with its extensive sandbanks.

For half an hour or more we steamed past a succession of buoys and met a good deal of incoming traffic. Then came the open sea, murky and rough enough to dash up over the top deck.

No one seemed to worry much. I found a foothold difficult and failed to secure my sea legs, so that I sat down and tried to read an inferior murder story. Jill with more success settled down to Vicki Baum's *Mustard Seed*.

I visited the bar for more whisky and ginger ale which did me no good. My stomach felt constricted, but I certainly never felt sick.

At six o'clock we ran into a gale and a cloudburst enveloped us, drenched us and hid all the seascape from view.

When it cleared I caught sight for the first time of the island, a long chain of hills, half hidden in the mist, looking not unlike the South Downs.

We were due in at Douglas at seven o'clock but it was 7.20 when we berthed in the rain. We got an elderly and wizened porter to transfer our baggage from the hold to a taxi and drove along the dock, then over the swing bridge to the white Fort Anne Hotel which stands in solitary state immediately above the harbour on the sides of a green down.

It is a Victorian house and has a happy atmosphere. Our room, number eleven, overlooks the harbour and the exquisite curve of Douglas Bay, which I have heard, with some justice, compared to Naples. At dinner, where we were given a window seat, we were waited on by a tall, pretty, black-haired Irish girl who smilingly told us that she was called Maureen and came from Longford, and by a tall head waiter who recognised me from days when he had waited on me at the Grand Hotel, Brighton. This made us feel at home right away.

We walked after dinner along the front where I was delighted to see that they retain the one-horse trams which even at that hour, nine o'clock, were being well patronised.

The sunken rock gardens that run parallel with the promenade were very colourful and attracted a good deal of attention from the crowds who were perambulating up and down. There were about a dozen small sailing boats racing round a buoy in the bay; and we saw excursion boats returning from Port Soderick and others that had put out from Douglas Bay, where lines are provided free by the boatmen for the mackerel fishing.

There was a large crowd dancing to Joe Loss's band in a rotunda, and Coronation flags still bedecked many of the scores of small hotels, Gresham, Cunard, Mona, Albany and so on that occupy the whole of the front.

There were still children building castles on the sand and paddling in the water, which was as clear as the Mediterranean but green, not blue, in colour.

The crowd was mixed. There were a large number of grizzled miners, all stockish and diminutive in height, several boys in obviously new suits and suede shoes with thick rubber soles ('demob' issues?) and pleasant, laughing young girls in print frocks. One elderly man in a Homburg and shining black boots, which I believe were elastic-sided, sat on a seat poring over a letter, and firemen were busy refilling a vast paddling pool with water pumped up from the sea.

The town fizzles out into a succession of white villas on the northern side where a high cliff encloses the bay. On the southern side the cliffs closely resemble those between Ilfracombe and Combe Martin.

We returned about ten o'clock and arranged with the night porter that he should produce some tea when I came down for it at four o'clock, instead of my having to ring down for it and so wake Jill.

Very tired, as I always am after a sea-voyage however short, I then went to bed and immediately to sleep.

WEDNESDAY   *Hall Caine's House—*
                          Tynwald Hill—Laxey—Ramsey

I was woken up at 4.30 by a loud ring on the telephone which also of course woke Jill. I reminded the night porter when he brought my tea up that I had asked him not to ring but had told him that I would come down for it. This is the first time that I have had to be woken up at four or thereabouts for over a year.

I sat in the window watching with joy the colours in the cloudy sky change from gold and lemon yellow to light green and grey while a two-funnelled steamer sailed silently out at five o'clock in a northerly direction.

Day excursions are run twice a week to Belfast (16/- return) and Dublin (18/- return) which sounds attractive, for days when the wind has dropped, but I rather think that these sailings are later, at 8.30, so I don't know where this ship was bound. There are also day excursions to Liverpool which enable the Islanders, early in the football season, to see First Division Football.

The sea gulls were noisy and scores of little sailing boats bobbed up and down in the wind-swept harbour.

After Cheltenham and Oxford I found the air tremendously invigorating but cold.

From my bedroom window I looked out on a ceiling of brilliantly tinted clouds, all orange and yellow. Steamers were flying flags and steam coming out of their funnels betokened preparations to depart. At breakfast I enjoyed my meal all the more watching late passengers scurry along the quay running at top speed in relays from 8.20 till 8.35, when *Mona's Queen* set sail for Liverpool.

Mr. Bond, who called for us at nine o'clock, is extremely knowledgeable and I find it difficult to remember a quarter of the many interesting things he told me.

Our hotel apparently stands on Irish soil, as its original builder married an heiress who only enjoyed her money if she lived on Irish soil, and in order, therefore, to fulfil the terms of this bequest, he brought over enough earth from Ireland to make the foundations for Fort Anne.

We drove out by way of the Nunnery, a large private house in a densely wooded park, the seat of the Fry-Goldie-Taubman family and full of heirlooms, to Kirk Braddan, where an open air service is held every Sunday which, Mr. Bond told us, attracted an enormous congregation.

There is a grandstand erected on the corner of the road here for spectators of the T.T. races. We passed into open country with several streams in which there was only a trickle of water, fields of well-looking cattle and sheep which I took to be Suffolk (they were not mountain sheep and they were too small to be Border-Leicesters). Hills rose on every side, two or three newly planted by the Manx Forestry Commission, and so we came to Hall Caine's house which is in charge of a caretaker. Close by is the house occupied by his adopted daughter. His own home ought to be converted into a museum, as it contains many literary relics, including Rossetti's sofa and a mantelpiece from Haworth.

Hall Caine's fate seems to be identical with that of Marie Corelli.

Over-praised and devoured in their life-time, they are now under-valued and not read at all. The younger generation do not even know the name of Hall Caine, and *The Deemster*, which sold in millions, now doesn't sell at all.

We got further reminders of Deemsters when, following the road through the Central Valley, we reached Tynwald Hill at St. Johns, where the main roads east and west, north and south bisect each other. The hill is a circular grassy mound in three tiers on a village green, which has a church at the eastern end. Mr. Bond stopped to tell us something of the Tynwald ritual.

It was a Norse custom to hold an annual open air assembly of all the freemen at some central point where changes in the law were announced, and disputes settled. Every freeman had a right to express his opinion or present his grievances.

This assembly was called the Thing, or Tyn. Wald is Norse for field. The meeting is held every Tynwald Day, 5th July. The mound on which it is convened is much older than the Norse invasion and was probably a burial ground of the Bronze Age.

A fair had originally been held on Midsummer Day, but when Christianity came to the island, the fair was linked with the name of St. John the Baptist whose festival is celebrated on 24th June. With the change in the calendar in the 18th century, the date was altered to 5th July.

The Lieutenant-Governor takes the central seat, once occupied by the Norse King, and by his side sits the Bishop of Sodor and Man.

In front sit the Deemsters and members of the Legislative Council and on the tier below sit the twenty four members of the House of Keys. At their feet sit the Vicars

The Harbour, Douglas

Country Road near St. John's

and Captains of Parishes, and outside the mound are the Freemen. There are two Deemsters, and it has been their duty to declare to the King what the laws were.

The House of Keys, chosen originally from the chief landowners, approximates to the House of Commons and decides what the law is and now makes new laws.

Before the Tynwald ceremony begins, the Court is fenced. The chief Coroner or Crownman, the Coroner of Glenfaba Sheading, reads out a notice warning people not to quarrel, brawl or make any disturbance. The original custom of roping off the mound has been abandoned. The present 'fencing' is imaginary.

'Sheadings' are the electoral districts for the return of sixteen of the twenty-four members of the House of Keys. They originally corresponded with the chief tribal units of the island. There were formerly sixteen parishes (now there are seventeen) each (with the exception of the parish of Marown) having a frontage on the sea board, each containing a church, selected from one of a number of Keeills or chapels in the area.

There used to be a subdivision of land known as 'treen', a small unit varying from 200 to 400 acres, each of which had its own Keeill. In Norse days each treen had to supply four fully equipped men to serve in the war galleys.

It was while we were looking at the Tynwald mound that Mr. Bond reminded me that the Manx people have no uniform appearance. Some are very dark, some are very fair. They are a mixture of Nordic and Mediterranean races.

We stopped to look at a roofless church in a field, roofless because the local fairies decided that they didn't want a roof and would only allow the building to go on if a certain tailor sat in the church all night and made a pair of trousers fit for fairies to wear. He obviously failed to satisfy their demands.

Bond showed us a hill on the southern side of the road

down which witches used to be rolled in barrels, the inside of which were lined with sharp protruding nails. Witch burning was apparently never a popular island sport as it was in Lancashire.

I was struck by the number of cosy-looking one-storeyed white-washed cottages which are, however, no longer thatched as they used to be.

We arrived at the city of Peel to see a good deal of activity at the end of the pier where people were fishing in large numbers. This is a favourite haunt of mackerel and conger eel. In the harbour we saw scores of drifters but only three of them bore the Peel mark. Most of them were Leith boats.

"Herring fishing is a hard life," said Mr. Bond, "and precarious. One night the men may take £50 or £60 as their share of the spoil, another night they may take nothing. As the older fishermen retire, the younger men have found it more profitable to find occupations ashore."

I saw a number of fishermen sitting on benches at a corner called (I don't know why) 'the Kremlin', overlooking the harbour.

We called at one fish curing factory and were shown round by a Scot who thought that I was H. V. Morton.

As the wind had been too high for the drifters to go out there was no curing going on, but we were shown one or two very intricate machines, which gutted and cleaned the herrings at the speed of fifteen a second, or it may have been a minute. We saw the brine baths of deep khaki colour in which they were salted and then we saw them hanging on carefully smoked wooden poles hanging above slow oak-chip fires where each herring stays for some fifteen to twenty-four hours, until it becomes what we recognise as a kipper.

Elsewhere (Norway for example) they are varnished and emerge red and yellow and mahogany in colour. The

Manx kippers are the most tasty because they are small and smoked with extreme care.

They produce about six million kippers a year from the Peel factories and it is universally acknowledged that they are the finest in the world.

We had a considerable wait at the level crossing which gave me the chance to revive a childhood acquaintance with the fascinating toy engines and Victorian carriages that I had known and loved when I came to the island as a small boy.

We took time off for a drink and I found to my great joy that the licensing hours are from 11 a.m. till 11 p.m., which strikes me as much more sensible than the English hours. On Sundays you cannot drink at all: and they appear very strict about this.

We drove home by a different route, by way of narrow lanes with high banks of ferns and fuchsias that reminded me of Devon. Luckily we encountered no cars coming the other way, or we should have had to back for several yards. On the top we saw a deserted lead-mine and in the valley near St. John's a flourishing tweed mill. We passed the two rivers from which Douglas takes its name, the Dhu (black), sluggish, and the Glass, a little more lively but now containing very little water.

Mr. Bond told us of the Bird Sanctuary on the Calf of Man, which can only be reached by boat from Port St. Mary, the warden of which likes the isolation of his present position. In occupying it, he is said to have achieved a lifelong ambition.

He said that there was a great dearth of trees in the island except in the glens, but to my eye there seemed a reasonable number. The Isle of Man Forestry Board are doing their best to remedy the deficiency.

We passed miles of excellent grazing land and some good-looking fields of oats. The island's main product is grain.

We were held up by a healthy-looking flock of Suffolk sheep. There are a few Cheviot sheep on the hills, and some Border-Leicesters in the valleys, but I saw none.

The island is completely free of snakes—the influence of St. Patrick, no doubt—and there are no foxes. The tailless Manx cat still exists, but not in great numbers: a society to protect the breed has recently been formed. I had only seen three of these cats so far. However, as we whizzed by a row of cottages, here was another.

"Would you like a close look at one?" asked my escort.

By the time we had stopped and backed up the road, the cat had found shelter inside the cottage, which was its home. Not daunted by this, we knocked at the door and asked to see the cat. A rather unusual request, it occurred to me. I wondered what my reception of any such visitor would have been if this had happened to me while engaged in my daily chores.

However, the elderly cottager who opened the door showed no dismay. He was as Manx as the cat and it was clearly a bond between them. The cat was an intimate member of the family and had quite a story which I only barely understood. Moreover, it had a kitten. The mother was a tortoise-shell and the kitten black and they were put on the small stretch of pavement to do their paces. I could soon see the point of this, as its taillessness is only one feature of the Manx cat. The other is the extra length of the hind quarters and hind legs, which move together instead of alternately, so that when the cat moves forwards it hops like a rabbit instead of strolling as other cats throughout the world do. As our small black kitten hopped up and down in front of us, one could well credit the theory that the Manx cat owed its origin to a cross between a cat and a rabbit that, for some reason unknown to our biologists, took place originally on the Calf of Man. I only wish that Imogen had been with us to see it.

There has also been on the Island a breed of tailless sheep.   There is also a Manx hen which has no tail feathers, but she is rare. I certainly didn't see her. I have the feeling that she may be apocryphal.

The industry of the island seems to be divided between tourism, curing kippers and agriculture. The lead mines, once a source of prosperity, are now deserted. Though I believe there are schemes for starting them again with modern equipment. There are five tweed mills in the island.

I keep on being reminded of Devon by the amount of fuchsia, the heather on the uplands and the ferns that line the high hedges in the narrow lanes.

As we repassed the Nunnery, we were reminded of an old romance connected with it. A young subaltern called Fry fell in love with the heiress, one of the Goldie-Taubmans. At first the family disapproved. But in later years her husband became the Governor of the Island, whereupon, I imagine, that they relented. Anyway, the family is now known as Fry-Goldie-Taubman.

After luncheon Mr. Bond called for us and drove us by way of the promenade to the northern cliffs, which are quite wild and lovely, but not improved by a series of amusement parks—though there is the compensating advantage that these are well clear of the town.

The Majestic, a luxury hotel on the north cliff, has an open-air swimming pool which looked inviting had it not been so windy.

We continually diverged from the wide main road to explore by-lanes of extreme narrowness and to enjoy views of coves and sea-cliffs. Everywhere white cottages nestle into the sides of wooded combes.

Soon we came to Laxey, which lies in a deep gully and wears a rather derelict look as it was once a prosperous lead-mining centre.

There is a harbour and there were crowds of tourists wandering vaguely in the middle of the road or lying on the grassy banks that lined the road that led up to the famous Laxey wheel. This was built in 1854 by a local engineer for the purpose of operating the pumps which freed the neighbouring lead-mines from water. At that time it was the largest wheel in the world, thanks to its circumference of 226 feet, and was highly efficient for its purpose. However, now it seemed somewhat smaller than even I remembered it and, as I looked at the rather old-fashioned crankshafts and the wooden sluices and conduits at the side, I was irresistibly reminded of the ingenious devices drawn by Heath Robinson who, for all one knows, has got many of his inspirations from these enterprising Victorian engineers. The solid, white stone tower at the side of the wheel enhances this impression and visitors were climbing up and down the spiral staircase on the outside of this.

It must be a money-maker for its owner, as the crowd was terrific.

The village, though having no special attraction, does, however, lie in the neighbourhood of several quite enchanting glens, one of which, Ballaglass, we explored. In its whole length we only met two walkers, which surprised me, as it contains a crystal clear stream that tumbles over great boulders and is lined with ancient thick trees of great beauty. This glen is, moreover, the property of the Manx National Trust and is, therefore, free and well-cared for with easy paths that have been especially cut out, with steps and wooden rails.

Glen Ballaglass joins Glen Mona to merge into a bay that is very like Woody Bay on Exmoor.

We stopped to inspect a deserted thatched one-storeyed cottage with but and ben, just like the 'black' houses of the Outer Hebrides.

There was a cock loft where the children slept and two

main downstairs rooms. These derelict cottages are usually taken over by the fairies, so they are never pulled down.

The most interesting thing I saw that afternoon was the Cashtel yn Ard, a fine megalith superbly situated below the mountains and above the sea cliffs, right off the beaten track close by a clump of fir trees. It consists of several massive stones, phallic in design, with a hole, on the other side of which lay seven cists or burial grounds in a row. Beyond this again stands an altar, the stones of which are discoloured. It is presumed that this is due to the burning of the bodies before burial. I saw and heard no bird, but Mr. Bond, who had spent the early years of his life in Laxey, said that he usually heard the cuckoo here. It is an eerie beautiful place in a wilderness of foxgloves and is almost entirely unvisited.

The Manx Archaeological Society have gone to infinite trouble to replace fallen and removed stones to their original foundations.

When we rejoined the main road we passed a fine-looking house on the top of a steep hill, called 'Rest and Be Thankful', which was formerly a posting house for coaches.

Then we descended to Ramsey Bay and looked out over the flat and fertile Point of Ayre, the northernmost corner of the island, beyond which we saw quite clearly the hills of Dumfries, which are less than eighteen miles away over the sea.

Ramsey was much more deserted than I remembered it of old. It has a vast stretch of sands, but I only saw one bather. It has a long pier where Queen Victoria once landed and there is a tower on the hill above which commemorates a view that particularly pleased the Prince Consort.

Ramsey is a roomy town with plenty of tall hotels and boarding houses and a fine public park and golf course, tennis courts and colourful gardens. It was occupied by the Royal Navy and Royal Air Force during the war, when boarding-house keepers turned their houses into flats under the impression that the Services were there permanently.

They lost touch with their regular clients in this way.

It is a rather exposed town, grand in hot sunny weather, but not so attractive when the wind blows. The place seemed to be mainly in the possession of kilted boys from a Scottish youth camp.

It is so proud of its reception of Queen Victoria that it still styles itself 'Royal Ramsey'.

We drove back by the inland mountain road which is part of the T.T. course. Near the summit of the hill we passed a monument to Jimmy Guthrie, one of the most fearless English riders, who was killed in a motorcycle race in Germany in 1937.

The road runs right up to the shoulder of Snaefell, a green smooth mountain with peat beds, but otherwise unexciting except for its magnificent views. It is a lonely land, with scarcely a house in sight most of the way. The road is almost hedgeless and open to all the storms and winds that blow.

The road rises to a height of 1500 feet and then descends quickly into Douglas by way of the Boys' High School and the starting point and finishing post of the T.T. races to Douglas.

*   *   *

After dinner we walked up to the cliffs at the back of the hotel, which are not improved by Camera Obscura, fun fairs and bars. There is a fine track along the cliff edge to Port Soderick, with a massive and very ugly Victorian brick toll gate which is derelict. Also derelict is the old railed track which was taken over by the Navy in the war and allowed to get into such a state of disrepair that the bridges over the deep gullies, have had to be fenced off and steps round made for walkers. No motors can get along. These cliffs are now the haunt of gulls, as the sea below is of lobsters.

THURSDAY *Douglas—The Museum—*
Bathing Beauty Competition

This was very much my Social Day, what the Victorians would have called an At Home Day.

At the end of it, though my duties were trivial, I found myself even more than ever in sympathy with Queen Elizabeth, who at the time of the Coronation was the cynosure of eyes in England, Scotland, Ireland and Wales, conferring upon countless thousands (millions if you include television) the blessing of her presence and happy smile.

During these six weeks the stock of Britain soared so high that we who are partakers in this change are unable to realise it or compute its worth.

It reflects itself, quite definitely, in the crowds that throng the Douglas Front. I'm sure that I am not imagining this. I have seen less manifestations of holiday fretfulness, and more genuine if rather quiet happiness, than I have seen for years. Allow, of course, that we have had time for war neuroses to quieten down, allow of course, that the removal of restrictions have played their part. I still firmly believe that the Coronation is mainly responsible for this extremely happy situation. We seem, somehow, to have come much closer together as a people.

It is usual, for instance, in an hotel of this sort, which I take to be the luxury hotel of the island, for some visitors to throw their weight about, at any rate to appear not to notice the existence of their fellow men.

Here, in spite of being elderly, and therefore with the

excuse of being crotchety, they are affable without being too matey.

Perhaps the standard is set by the staff, all of whom smile and greet us as if they were really glad to open doors for us and wait on us at table. There is an elderly man who usually wears an Old Rugbeian or it may be an Old Cliftonian tie (I never can distinguish between those colours) who is the possessor of a wife and a Scottie who are all very friendly.

The majority of the Fort Anne visitors have their own cars, and spend their time fishing, playing golf or exploring the island. The hotel is essentially Victorian in architecture, and the rooms are spacious with high ceilings and huge windows that provide so good a view of the harbour that we are tempted to spend the day and a great part of the night just sitting watching the traffic below.

I am continually surprised by the activity. At one period today I saw no fewer than seven of those staunch one-funnelled black and red steamers lying up. They steal in and out of the harbour unfussily and with very occasional hooting. The little sailing boats from Port St. Mary have been marooned here for several days as the wind is too high to allow of their making for home.

There are cargo boats, and very frequently a long string of rowing boats being towed in crocodile round the end of the harbour towards the shore and back again. There are well over a hundred of these. There are ferries and speed-boats and even an occasional drifter, though the majority of drifters tie up in Peel harbour where the curing factories are.

From the weather point of view today was very odd. The high hills were shrouded with heavy rain clouds, but the rain never reached Douglas where the sun shone brilliantly throughout the day, so brilliantly that I was astonished to read in the evening paper that it was raining in Manchester so much that the Test Match started late and had to be interrupted.

The Australians had made 81 for 3 by tea time, when it was still raining.

I tasted my first Manx kippers at breakfast. They were small but delicious. At luncheon I had my first Manx lobsters, caught this morning. They were as succulent as any lobsters I have ever eaten. The other outstanding island delicacy is the Manx cheese which is mild but in some respects as good as Wensleydale cheese.

I was called for at 9.30 and I left Jill to spend the morning typing my book reviews and other articles while I made a round of courtesy visits.

I met Mr. Barwell, who had sent us a pass for all entertainments, and Mr. Perry, an Old Eastbourne College boy who is in charge of the Villa Marina where Jack Leon's orchestra plays in the gardens during the day and Joe Loss and his orchestra plays in the vast rotunda at night. The hall is to be used for the forthcoming T.U.C. conference and already men are busy making provision for the requirements of the B.B.C. and television engineers.

We drove up to the Museum, which is a modern, light and handsomely-appointed building with very interesting maps of the island, where I studied with some care the geological section which shows an astonishingly variety of strata, granite, slate, red sandstone, limestone, grit, marl and almost every known form of stone, all violently disturbed by glacial movement.

I met the director, Mr. Megaw, who reminded me of the fact that I had met his father (in Belfast) who writes under the name of Arthur Stanley.

There have been Cistercian monks in the island, and the Nunnery is still the island's outstanding house, though it has passed into the hands of a private family. But the Catholics are not prominent, and though there are a number of churches of no outstanding architectural beauty, the Nonconformists are numerically by far the most numerous denomination.

We called at the Governor's house, a fine building high up above the town set among trees commanding a magnificent view over the town and bay, where I signed the visitors' book but did not see Sir Ambrose Dundas Flux Dundas, who is about to go on leave.

Then we went on to the Mayor's Parlour, where the Mayor, a very affable and pleasant person who is a yeast merchant, showed me the Council Chamber, a solid, light oak-panelled room with photographs of his predecessors set on the panels all round the chamber. He is ambitious for the island to top the million a year mark for visitors, which means an influx of 50,000 visitors a week for twenty weeks. At present, Douglas, with a resident population of 25,000, attracts a weekly total of about 30,000, the majority of whom are content to lie on the grass on the promenade, relax in deck chairs in the gardens or sit on the beach.

We called on Mr. Andrew Douglas, General Manager of the Steam Packet Company, in an office very similar to the shipping offices in Threadneedle Street, and I got some insight into the complexities of a highly efficient and very busy organisation.

The influence of the North in its brisk business attitude to life is very marked and is obviously due to the infiltration of the Scottish element.

The island breed is very mixed.

The Viking conquest superimposed upon the native Celt a certain vigour but it is noteworthy that, as in England at the Norman conquest, the conqueror did not impose his language. Certain Scandinavian root words are to be found in the Manx language, but the earlier Gaelic remained as the spoken language, and Manx, which is still spoken by a few islanders and is perpetuated by the printing of a Manx Bible and Manx dictionary, is essentially Gaelic in origin. It has many ballads and songs, and even Aesop's Fables have been translated.

The Manx emigrate almost to the same extent that the Irish do. Just as the Orcadians export eggs and brains, so do the Manx export kippers and brains. Wherever they go, they succeed in all branches of life and their numbers multiply. I heard it said—though I will not vouch for the truth of this—that there are more Manxmen in Cleveland, Ohio, than there are in the Isle of Man, these being the descendants of the lead miners who emigrated there in the eighteen forties.

Be this last statement true or not, I have been interested to read in the time I have been revising this book the account of the meeting of the North American Manx Association, held in Cleveland in August, which was attended by the enterprising and successful Mr. T. R. Radcliffe, Editor-in-Chief of the *Isle of Man Examiner*. This association has almost one thousand members scattered throughout the United States and Canada and holds its conventions periodically at different cities throughout that Continent. The meeting this year is the twenty-fifth anniversary of the formation of the Association in the late nineteen-twenties as an outcome of a visiting party from the homeland, of which Mr. Radcliffe was also a member. I see that one of the visits on this occasion was to the Manx grave plot in the Highland Park Cemetery, this being a plot provided many years ago by the Mona's Relief Society, it being a point of pride that no Manxman should ever have to be buried in a pauper's grave.

An interesting suggestion was made by Mr. Radcliffe that the Cleveland radio network should introduce a special programme on Tynwald Day, as is the custom in both Australia and New Zealand.

The Manx system of education is bilateral and does not come under the Ministry of Education in Whitehall. Today, there is a High School for Girls at one end of the town and a High School for Boys at the other. They are, however, both integral parts of the Douglas High Schools and administered as one unit.

In the afternoon I was called upon to judge a Bathing Beauties Competition, and prepared a speech pleading for a Beauty Competition for men of my sort, old and fat, but was relieved to find that it was my judgment, not my facetiousness, that was required.

A crowd of some five thousand visitors basked quietly and contentedly in deck chairs on sloping lawns and listened to a native crooner singing 'A Bushel and a Peck' to Jack Leon's band as a preliminary, before the fourteen competitors appeared to fascinate us with their smiles and curves.

They were a pleasant unassuming group of girls, all but one well shaped, with rather large thighs, firm shapely legs, neat shining hair, and two (to my surprise) with shining unpowdered faces. Their hands showed signs of honest work. I forgot to see whether their nails were painted red (a habit that I, in common with most men, abhor).

I had less idea of the points that I was supposed to look for than if I had been called upon to judge a Beagle Puppy show. But what I soon realised was that I was to be given far less time than if I had been judging puppies. This struck me as unfair.

I could have gazed on these comely girls for a long time without discomfort, but all they did was to come singly down a short platform towards me, dazzle me with their smile (all but one who remained obstinately poker-faced), then file off and come back in reverse order, before standing in a row for final judgment. I gathered that deportment was an asset, but otherwise I found myself concentrating on their faces (I gave a lot of marks to simplicity and geniality) and legs, with much less emphasis on their curvaceousness. I am a little bashful about gazing at girls' breasts. I don't know why. I felt that my own twenty-two-year-old daughter Lalage would have failed to secure any marks by reason of her slimness. All these girls were plump. At one moment I felt almost that I was selecting chickens for lunch.

The girl I spied first (last on the list) immediately fascinated me with her naturalness. She was smaller than the others, about 5 feet 7 inches tall, with black, rather unruly hair, extremely attractive glowing grey-green eyes, well-knit body and a girlish manner that immediately pleased me. She became my number one and had no rivals.

My second selection was a very different type, quite obviously a professional model, stream-lined, debonair, soignée, with carefully brushed hair worn in a bun, who carried herself superbly, if rather condescendingly. I didn't feel drawn to her as a person, I felt no inclination to make a date with her or ask her to dance as I did with number one, but she undoubtedly had beauty. She was the only one who was married.

My third selection was a merry-faced, fair-haired girl with an enchanting dimple, who had me in her toils at once because of her smile. I was too fascinated by her face to take much notice of her body beyond realising that she was well-shaped, had good sturdy legs and was decidedly a person. The rest were more or less obvious also-rans, so I didn't expect to be lynched by the crowd for a wrong decision when, after comparing notes and marks with Jill to find she had chosen the same girls in the same order, I announced the results which indeed seemed to meet with the approval of the vast crowd.

What did surprise me was the origin of my choice. Two

out of three were local, the winner from Ramsey, the third from Douglas. The professional came from Cheshire. This struck me as significant. Quite by accident I had discovered that the Isle of Man breeds pretty girls. My two selections would stand out in any bevy of girls for their natural demeanour and good shape. Their features were regular, they were perhaps a shade shorter than the average girl, but they had good looks and great charm. They were completely unsophisticated.

I had to go on the stage and put a sash round the shoulders of the winner, while Jill presented envelopes to the second and third winners. After congratulating them, we went off to be photographed with them. It was then that I discovered where all the entrants came from.

I was surprised to find a girl from Brighton. One came from Peterborough, two from Cheshire, my two selections from the island and the rest from Lancashire.

They were all as easy to talk to as they were easy on the eye and I enjoyed my afternoon enormously.

At tea we were entertained by a group of aldermen, one of whom had brought his binoculars, and pressmen. One of the pressmen edits *Mona's Herald*, a weekly that is over a hundred years old.

We had tea in the very pleasant café above the Villa Marina dance hall and I was struck by the dressiness of the crowd.

On the Promenade and particularly on the steps of all the boarding houses and hotels, which get the full morning sun, men sit in open shirts and waistcoats, the girls in shorts and slacks, the older women in print frocks.

After tea Jill and I walked over the headland at the back of the hotel along the track that leads to Port Soderick. We only met one group of walkers, all Scots, footsore and very weary, returning from Port Soderick.

We looked down over precipitous cliffs to see gulls

hugging the ledges and lobster pots in great profusion in the deep, clear, green water. Larks sang overhead among the thickets on the Downs above.

It is astonishing how quickly you leave the great milling mass of Douglas visitors behind. They obviously have no inclination to walk.

I was so sleepy after dinner that my attempts to read Kinvig's History of the Isle of Man were soon abandoned. After a siesta in the lounge, I went upstairs to look out on the steamer bringing back the Manx farmers from the Royal Show at Blackpool, watched the Promenade brilliantly lit up and went to my bath and bed about ten to sleep more soundly than I have slept for many months.

FRIDAY

The House of Keys—Castle Rushen
Castletown—Port St. Mary—
Cregneish—The Calf of Man

The gale, which had been so high for about a week that Canadian-bound liners from Liverpool couldn't sail, today moderated and then faded out altogether. It was a sunny and warm day over here but again rained hard enough in Manchester to put a stop to play in the Test Match.

After a memorable breakfast of four kippers, I went down with Jill to see Mr. Fick, the Assistant General Manager of the Isle of Man Steam Packet Company. He told me that they had put into commission no less than five new passenger ships since the war, which struck me as a great act of courage and optimism.

In 1947 they built the *King Orry* (*IV*), 2485 tons and *Mona's Queen* (*IV*), 2485 tons, *Tynwald* (*V*), 2493 tons, in 1948 *Snaefell* (*V*), 2489 tons, and in 1951 *Mona's Isle*.

Four ships were lost in the war, three at Dunkirk. Eleven ships have been sold since 1930. There are now nine ships in commission, the oldest, *Viking*, now nearly fifty years old. These ships have brought over an average of well over half-a-million visitors every year (excluding the war years) since 1920, the highest number being in 1948, when nearly 590,000 passengers came to the island by sea.

Well over 100,000 now come by air each year, and a sharp rise is expected in these numbers since the opening of the new airport in June, 1953.

These ships are all staffed by Manx-born officers and men, and bring visitors from Liverpool, Fleetwood, Ardrossan, Dublin, Belfast and Heysham. The Isle of Man Steam Packet Company was founded in 1830.

We spent practically the whole morning in the House of Keys with the Speaker, Mr. Qualtrough, a man of my own age, sixty-eight, whom I found to be most knowledgeable on every aspect of island life. He is, of course, most interested in the political and economic system.

He took me over the building which contains three places of Assembly. The first was that of the House of Keys, which approximates to the House of Commons, with twelve seats and desks on either side of the Chamber and the Speaker's chair in the middle, equipped with a ram's horn containing a snuff-box. Next was the Assembly Room of the Legislative Council of eleven, which approximates to the House of Lords. Finally, we came to the Tynwald Court where the two houses come together under the chairmanship of the Governor.

The Legislative Council consists of the Governor, Bishop, two Deemsters, the Attorney General, four representatives of the House of Keys and two members nominated by the Governor who acts as Chancellor of the Exchequer and is, therefore, responsible for the Budget.

The island, which became very prosperous during the war, is now in such a tight place that there is a movement to increase the income tax from 5s. od., but this is not popular. The Speaker believes that prosperity comes from the circulation of money, but beyond the tourist traffic, agriculture and the export of kippers, there are no industries. He himself is a timber merchant, but now that timber is once again easily available from Finland he can't export it. While, on the island, building projects have had to come to a halt owing to a lack of funds everywhere.

The island badly needs more trees, but owing to the salt in the air many types of tree, lime, sycamore and firs don't flourish, and in any event, schemes of afforestation have had to be abandoned owing to a lack of money.

The Manx have their own system of laws and therefore have their own Bar exams, and barristers and solicitors are merged into one profession. There is no great crime wave, and there has been no murder for at least thirty years. There's a good deal of petty larceny, and juvenile delinquency is common as there are so many youths of sixteen or so with nothing to do once the season is over.

The main religious denomination is Methodism, but the Catholics, due to the influx of Irish domestic servants in the summer, are so numerous that there is a queue waiting for Mass every Sunday morning at 6, 7, 8, 9, 10 and 11 o'clock. There is, of course, an Established Church in every parish, but the greatest attendance by far is at the open-air service which is held every Sunday morning at Kirk Braddan, just outside the town.

There is a dearth of crafts and craftsmen. The Kelly brothers are outstanding wood workers and there are still a few dry stonewallers and thatchers left.

I was surprised to learn that there is not a Manx Artists' Colony. The best known artist is Hoggatt of Port Erin. Other Island painters are John Nicholson, Quayle, Archie Knox and Freddie Leach, but obviously there is no Artistic School comparable with that of Newlyn.

In the windows of one of the Chambers I saw the coats of arms of successive generations of rulers and Governors, among them those of the Stanley family. For several hundred years the Lord Derby of the period ruled over the island from Rushen Castle. The Speaker gave me a full history of the Armorial bearings of the Isle of Man.

THE ARMORIAL BEARINGS OF THE ISLE OF MAN

"It must be," said some wag, "to compensate for the fact that its cats have no tails that the Manx adopted as their coat of arms a man with three legs."

As a matter of fact it is not a man with three legs, but just the three legs of a man, and it provides one of the most interesting of all coats of arms, the meaning and origin of which give rise to endless speculation. It is easy, of course, to compare it with the swastika, which is one of the oldest and most universal of symbols. There is a pre-historic stone on Ilkley Moor which contains a crudely-inscribed design which might be either a swastika or the three legs of man.

The three legs symbol seems to have had its origin in Sicily. At any rate, it has been famous as a badge in that island from very early times. There is, for instance, an early fifth century B.C. vase discovered in Agrigentum, in Sicily, which depicts on one side a fierce fight between Achilles and Memnon for the possession of the body of Antilochus and on the other side Aurora, the mother of Antilochus, carrying away her dead son. On Memnon's shield is a very clear impression of the three legs.

The heraldic description of the Manx form is :

'Gules : three legs armed, conjoined in fesse at the upper part of the thighs, flexed in triangle, proper, garnished and spurred, or'.

The feet in the Sicilian device were booted and ran in a clockwise direction, but were not, as they are in the Manx coat of arms, spurred.

The motto, *Quocunque Jeceris Stabit*, means 'Whichever way you throw me I stand'.

The particular application of the device to the island has now lost its meaning, but the suggestion is that when England, Scotland and Ireland were at war with one another, the island's independence depended on preserving an armed neutrality, or on gaining the protection of one state against another. So the legs denote self-defence, the spurs (I don't know why) speed, and the point is that whichever way the symbol falls two of the legs will fall into an attitude of supplication while the third kicking upwards and behind shows its defensive attitude to the third power.

As they now stand, one knee is bent in homage towards England, one leg looks as if it were giving a vicious kick upwards at Southern Scotland and the third appears to be having a jab at Dublin.

This idea of the interpretation of the coat of arms is ingenious, but no more likely than the theory that the legs were a reminder of the Trinity or that they were a corruption of the blazing spokes of Thor's thunderbolt. The truth is that there is no satisfactory explanation of the choice of this particular coat of arms and no one knows how the symbol found its way from Sicily. Some say that it came by way of the Scandinavian Kings of Mann in the eleventh or twelfth century. It is known that the Norse Kings had close connections with Sicily.

Others say that it was introduced by Alexander III of Scotland, to whom the island was ceded in 1266. This sounds the more plausible, as Alexander was in attendance at the English court at the time when preparations were being made to enforce the claim of Henry III's son Edmund as King of Sicily. The Sicilian badge would undoubtedly be known in the English court and Alexander may well have appropriated it for his island kingdom.

At any rate, the seals of King Harald in 1245 and 1246 were decorated with a Viking ship and the first known use of the three legs was on the shield of Henry de Bello Monte, Lord of Mann in 1310. It was adopted again almost immediately afterwards when Thomas, Earl of Moray, took over the island from Robert the Bruce in 1313.

The three legs design is on the Sword of State which is carried in the Tynwald procession and housed in the Museum. The story that the Sword was used by Olaf Godredson against the Moors in Spain in 1215 lacks proof and even probability. The experts are by no means agreed.

The three legs are also inscribed on the village market cross at Maughold, the date of which is the late fourteenth century. So it has been the island's device for a good many centuries. The motto made its first appearance on Manx coins in 1668.

The Speaker showed me some of the old statutes. One of the most interesting was that known as the 'Rope, Sword or Ring'.

If a girl, who had been taken without her consent, bore a child without marriage, she was presented with the choice of a rope with which to hang the father, a sword with which to cut off his head or a ring with which to marry him. This struck me as a very sensible sort of law, but I was told of a case in which the girl elected to use the rope and then relented in favour of the ring when her man had been suspended. Once cut down, however, the man refused the ring, declaring that he had already been hung. "No man," said he, "can be punished twice for the same offence."

I was pleased with the phraseology of a plea concerning the constitution of the Tynwald which I reproduce :

CONSTITUTION OF TYNWALD

"Our Doughty and gracious Lord, this is the Constitution of Old time the which we have given in our days, how ye should be Govern'd on their Tynwald day. First you shall come thither in your Royal Array, as a King ought to do by the Prerogatives and Royalties of the Land of Man, and upon the Hill of Tynwald sit in a Chair, covered with a Royal Cloath and Quishions, and your visage unto the East, and your Sword before you, holden with the point upward, your Barons in the Third Degree sitting beside you, and your Beneficed Men, and your Deemsters before you sitting, and your Clerk, your Knights, Esquires, and Yeomen about you in the Third Degree, and the worthiest Men in your Land to be called in before your Deemsters, if you will ask anything of them, and to hear the Government of your Land, and your Will, and the Commons to stand without the Circle of the Hill with Three Clerks in their Surplices; and your Deemsters shall make call on your Coroner of Glanfaba, and he shall call in all the Coroners of Man, and their Yardes in their Hands with their weapons upon them, either Sword or Ax; and the Moars, that is to wit, of every Sheading: Then the Chief Coroner, that is the Coroner of Glanfaba, shall make a fence upon pain of Life or Lymme, that no Man make any disturbance or stir in the time of Tynwald, or any murmerer rising in the King's presence, upon a pain of hanging and drawing: And then shall let your Barons, and all other know you to be King and Lord; . . ."

There was a period during which the islanders expelled all the Scots and refused to let them enter as a result of the harsh rule of the island under Robert the Bruce. I was told, in fact, that it is still a law of the Isle of Man that a Scotsman may be shot at sight. Fortunately, these days this is more honoured in the breach than the observance. Indeed, the islanders today welcome all comers with open arms and strike me as being a peculiarly placid and amiable people who certainly show no resentment at the wholesale invasion by the Lancastrian hordes of today.

After lunch we were taken by Mr. Bond's assistant,

Mr. Cottier, to the Ronaldsway Air Terminal, a splendid and ultra modern building which was only opened in June 1953. It occupies a wide flat area close by the sea, adjoining King William's College, just outside Castletown. Its aerial advantage is that it is not only the hub of the North, but the exact centre of the British Isles. This explains the many services running. Liverpool, London, Glasgow, Manchester and Belfast are served by B.E.A., Birmingham and Blackpool by Lancashire Aircraft Corporation, Carlisle, Glasgow and Newcastle by Manx Airlines, Dublin by Aer Lingus, Prestwick by Scottish Airlines, Newcastle by B.K.S. Aerocharters and Roberts' Tours and Wolverhampton by Don Everall (Aviation).

There was a tremendous coming and going and from the Control Room I watched two B.E.A. planes take off for Northolt. The in traffic returns for 1952 were 128,310. In one month of that year, 32,494 passengers passed through the airport and in one week-end 5,792 passed through.

After leaving the Airport we passed King William's College and stopped at Castle Rushen, Castletown. As the whole of Manx history for the last six hundred years seems to be bound up in Castle Rushen it is worth while tracing its development in detail. It is commonly agreed that it is one of the best preserved castles in existence. This is largely due to the work of a former Governor, Lord Raglan.

There was originally a stockade built above the inlet of the sea and the Manx called the town Balla Cashtal, meaning the homestead round the castle.

The castle is built entirely of a light carboniferous limestone quarried locally at Scarlett. It consists of the usual central keep, surrounded by a curtain wall and fortified gateway.

The buildings belong to four periods :—

(1) The square tower, built originally between 1150 and

1200 was destroyed by Robert the Bruce in 1313 and then rebuilt.

(2) The rebuilt central tower with three side towers, the curtain wall and portcullis gate, all the work of Sir William de Montacute and his son, between 1340 and 1360.

(3) Further fortifications to resist cannon fire built by the third Earl of Derby about 1540.

(4) The Derby family's additions of domestic buildings built by the seventh and later Earls.

Other architectural alterations were later made to convert it in turn into a prison, an asylum, a barracks and a house of legislation.   It is still used as a Court of Justice.

I was surprised to hear, in view of its stout defences, that it was not meant to be a menace to the surrounding country or even a fortress, but rather a safe haven or port for the visiting King of Mann, who could use it as a landing place for troops.   At any rate, it strikes the modern eye as a very substantial and indeed forbidding fortress.

There are three concentric rings of fortifications.   Inside is the Central Keep or Inner Ward with a portcullis and drawbridge.   Surrounding this, and separated from it by a deep gully, is the Main Ward, or curtain wall with the only gateway, and round the outside was a sloping grassy glacis, except on the harbour side where it was unnecessary.

I expected to find the castle built on a rock, but in point of fact its foundation is a mass of boulder clay.

We entered by the gatehouse, which has a guard-room and kitchen with a vaulted basement in which prisoners were formerly incarcerated.   Facing the Inner Ward, with its huge portcullis and drawbridge, stands the causeway on which the drawbridge was lowered.   Here are the ruins of the small oratory chapel added by the seventh Earl of Derby.

To the left of the gatehouse stands the extraordinarily ugly and incongruous looking Derby House, a three-storeyed building, faced with plaster, which is now occupied by the caretaker.

In the Main Ward are still traces of the workshops, stables, granaries, bakehouse, forge and Mint, which give a good indication of the castle's capacity to sustain a prolonged siege and to be self-supporting.

The Inner Ward still stands in its entirety as it has stood for eight hundred years, but it was completely enclosed by the fourteenth century building of Sir William de Montacute.

It has to be remembered that the Keep was equipped to maintain a garrison as well as the Lord.

The rooms, of which there are a great many, were originally reached by a narrow, stone spiral staircase, but in order to provide access for visitors today modern staircases have been added.

The first thing that struck me as I climbed into and out of the various rooms was their general air of gloom.

On the top of the outside stairs are the kitchen and dining-hall. There is a large fireplace in the kitchen, which is unusually small. The hall has no fireplace and is singularly plain. Beyond the dais end lies the withdrawing-room, which has a fireplace but which is exceptionally dark and grim. The most outstanding feature about it is the floor, which consists of very cold-looking slate rafters, each about a foot wide, twelve feet long and five inches thick.

On the floor above is an upper dining-room, now used as a Museum, and this, too, has a withdrawing-room.

I was most of all interested in the coats of arms of all the Kings and Lords of Mann which hang on the walls of many of the rooms and which help a little to lighten the general air of darkness.

The reason for the different halls and drawing-rooms was that three grades of Society occupied the Castle. The garrison fed in the guard-house, the minor officials with the household and garrison officers dined in the lower hall, and the Governor, Receiver-General, Comptroller, Water Bailiff, Attorney-General and Captain-General dined in the same hall as the Lord, but below the dais.

A decree was issued in 1422 that nobody might sit at the Lord's table unless he received what was oddly termed a 'Gentleman's Wages'.

The old oratory chapel is now used to house the famous clock which bears Queen Elizabeth's initials and is supposed, without much warrant, to have been presented by her during the period when she was Lord of Mann.

There is also a garrison chapel on the upper floor and more rooms for the garrison on the tops of the towers.

I got a glorious view over land and sea from the towers, which are quite easy to climb, and neither so high nor so capacious as I expected. They provide an admirable look-out, but do not allow room for more than a handful of sentries at once. What we do get from looking down on the Castle itself is a realisation of its amazing thick walls and great strength. Only treachery from within could possibly have caused this mighty fortress to have been taken by force before the days of heavy artillery.

Castle Rushen is associated with the history of the Stanley family who became Lords of Mann in 1405. John Stanley I never came to the island, but his successor, John Stanley II, who succeeded in 1414, not only visited it but took a great interest in it. It was he who introduced written laws, curbed the power of the Church and restored the original constitution.

The Bishop and barons were summoned by him to attend a Tynwald to pay obeisance to their new ruler, and when three of them failed to appear he deprived them of their lands in the island.

He codified the laws, and the Deemsters and Keys drew

up a sort of Magna Carta defining the rights and duties of King, Church and people for the first time. Before this the laws had been handed down orally and depended on the memory of the Deemsters and Keys. Trial by jury was substituted for trial by combat, and this member of the Stanley family was a beneficent ruler. He was followed by generations of Stanleys, who, for a hundred years, never visited their little kingdom.

However, in 1507 Thomas Stanley, the second Earl, gave up the title of King and became Lord of Mann, and came over in person to quell a public tumult. It was this visit that caused Derbyhaven to receive its name. The third Earl reigned from 1521 till 1572. During his term of office the Reformation took place and the queer thing is that, in spite of the fact that the law about the suppression of Monasteries did not extend to the island, the Manx monasteries were suppressed and their property seized by the Crown soon after those in England fell.

The Reformation was slow to take effect in the island because the third Earl was an ardent Catholic. The isolation of the island also played its part.

When the fifth Earl died Queen Elizabeth took over the control of the island as there was a dispute about his successor, and it wasn't until 1612 that the Stanleys came into their own again, when the sixth Earl and his Countess, Elizabeth, ruled jointly. Neither of them visited the island, but their son, Lord Strange, afterwards seventh Earl of Derby, took over in 1642, and he became by far the most influential of all the long line of Stanley rulers.

James Strange, known as the Great Stanley, was only twenty-one when he took over the rule of the island, and he showed his strong individuality by electing, for the first time in the island's history, a Manxman, Edward Christian of Maughold, as his Lieutenant-Governor. Christian had been a captain in the East India Company, a courtier in the suite of the Duke of Buckingham and a commander of a naval frigate. He had retired with a fortune to his native island and acquired the lead mine workings at Bradda Head, obviously a man of parts. He was described by his lord as "excellent company, as rude as a sea captain should be, but refined as one that hath civilised himself half a year at court". He declared himself to be content to give his services without payment, but in point of fact he was dismissed in 1639 because, according to the Earl, "the more I gave, the more he asked".

When the Civil War broke out, the Earl, who was an ardent Royalist, raised an army of 5,000 men, equipped at his own expense, and also gave Charles I large sums of money, in addition to rendering important services in the field. The odd thing is that, in spite of this, Charles never trusted him, as he was presumed to have an eye on the throne.

The Manx people nursed a good number of grievances against their rulers and were, in the main, on the side of Parliament. Edward Christian was in command of the Manx forces and was accused of inciting the soldiers to rebel against the Earl. But there had been trouble about tithes and the Governor had invited each parish to send representatives to state their grievances to prevent an insurrection. But instead of sending representatives, the whole population were summoned by the sending round of the Muster Cross (*Crosh Vusta*) and they came bearing arms.

Christian tried to appease them by promising to give them a later hearing, but one of the agitators, William Garett of Sulby, declared that he and his fellow islanders would fight and die rather than pay any more tithes. Christian then promised to send for Lord Derby, who brought with him a troop of English cavalry. He was tactful enough to be affable, and the meeting of parish representatives was held and the grievances heard. The Earl then convened an assembly of officers, twenty-four Keys and four men from every parish, in Peel Castle to help him to bring about an equitable settlement. Edward Christian and the ring-leaders of the disturbances were present and it looked as if the meeting was likely to be a stormy one, but the Earl had his own methods with would-be rioters. "There were some," he afterwards said, "who saucily behaved themselves and of those I put some out of countenance with austere looking on them : troubling their discourse in seeming not to hear very well what they said and asking them to repeat the same : which astonished them so, that oft they did forget the matter they were about."

By these refreshingly unorthodox means the Earl not only kept the meeting under control, but induced the gathering to leave the settlement of all the grievances to him. Christian rose to call attention to some question that had been overlooked, but he was ruled out of order and the meeting came to an end.

The sequel was, to my mind, unexpected and odd. Christian was arrested and charged with treason. He was accused of trying to overthrow the Government, to make the House of Keys an elected body, to have Deemsters chosen every three years from the Keys and to impose a new oath to repeal all laws not in the interests of the people. The suggestion is that he would have declared openly for Cromwell and had a considerable island backing. He was imprisoned for life and fined a thousand marks. He stayed in gaol until the entry of the Parliamentarian forces into the island in 1651. Eight years later he was again imprisoned for plotting against the then Governor and he died in gaol in Peel Castle in 1661.

Meanwhile, the Earl temporarily satisfied the islanders' grievances by reducing tithes, but he created a far more serious grievance by abolishing the ancient rights of tenants to pass on their farms to their children or to dispose of them at will. He substituted a plan of leases by which no one could hold land for longer than three generations.

But it was, of course, his Royalist activities that made the seventh Earl the most famous of all the Stanley lords. He raised a troop of cavalry, formed seven camps, erected forts and earthworks and even equipped a small fleet which defeated five men-of-war and later defended the Calf of Man from an attack by three of Cromwell's ships. When Charles was executed, the Parliament offered to return his English estates to the Earl if he would surrender the island. His answer was characteristic. "If you trouble me with any more such messages I will burn the paper and hang the bearer." Whatever else he lacked he did not lack courage. When, in 1651, an attempt was made to place Charles II on the throne he took over three hundred Manx foot soldiers, but was attacked and overwhelmed near Wigan. He escaped to join the King's army and fight at Worcester, where he was captured. In spite of promises that his life would be spared, he was court-martialled and executed at Bolton in 1651.

He was a strange mixture of a man, but undoubtedly cast in the heroic mould. So was his wife, the famous Countess Charlotte. She had already defended Lathom House for two years against the forces of the Parliament and now, in 1651, she was left to defend Castle Rushen.

This is where another famous Christian, William, known as Illiam Dhone, not to be confused with Edward the Governor, comes into the picture. William was one of Lady Derby's principal officers, a major-general and the son of a Deemster.

When the news came of the Earl's capture, the islanders seized the opportunity to try to get their grievances remedied.

Eight hundred of them met at William Christian's house at Ronaldsway and took an oath to withstand the Countess until she yielded to their grievances. They were told that she had secretly sent to make conditions of peace which, from our knowledge of her character, sounds quite incredible, and that she was prepared to sell the islanders 'for twopence apiece'.

Christian thereupon seized all the forts except Rushen and Peel, and sent a message to the Roundhead commander, Colonel Duckenfield, offering to surrender the island on condition that the natives might continue to enjoy their lives and liberty.

Duckenfield besieged Castle Rushen, which was pretty well impregnable, and summoned the Countess to surrender, telling her that her husband was dead. The news so seriously affected her that she offered to surrender, but only on terms more suitable to a conqueror than to a defeated party. So Duckenfield had no alternative but to bring up his cannon and begin the attack.

There is no reason to suppose that he could ever have taken the castle by assault. His only chance was to starve the Countess into submission, but there was treachery within. Some members of the garrison made a breach in the walls and admitted the attackers to the outer ramparts, and some of the garrison sought to escape by leaping from the battlements.

It was, without doubt, the defection and disloyalty of William Christian that turned the scale and prevented the garrison from putting up a defence. Lady Derby had no alternative but to surrender, and the sole condition that she made was that the lives of the defenders should be spared and that she and her family should be allowed to go to England to plead their own cause with the Roundhead leaders.

Christian's defence for his desertion of the Countess was that, if she had been encouraged and helped to continue resistance, there would have been needless bloodshed, and the islanders would have lost their ancient liberties.

It looks to me very much as if Christian's aim was to change the island's rulers. In any event, they were no better off under the Commonwealth, because Lord Fairfax, to whom Cromwell gave the island, continued to rule it on similar lines to that of the Stanley regime. Indeed, he appointed a Governor, James Chalenor, who accused William Christian of being short in his accounts, as a result of which he retired to his estates in Lancashire.

As the Commonwealth rule brought none of the reforms that the islanders had hoped for and expected, it is not altogether surprising that the Restoration of Charles II was hailed, at any rate in Peel, Castletown, Douglas and Ramsey with as general delight as it was on the mainland.

Charles Stanley, eighth Earl of Derby, was appointed Lord of Mann and immediately set about revenging himself on those who had betrayed his mother, especially, of course, William Christian.

Christian had been a prisoner for debt in London, but after his release he came back to the island believing that the general pardon by Charles II to his former enemies extended to the Isle of Man. He soon found out his mistake. The Earl had him arrested and brought to trial on the ground that the royal pardon did not cover offences committed against the Lord of Mann. Christian denied the right of the court and refused to plead and when several members of the House of Keys refused to condemn him they were removed.

So he was condemned to death really without trial. He appealed to the King in Council, but the appeal did not reach London until after he had been shot on Hango Hill. He made a deeply moving and eloquent valedictory speech in which he declared that he had acted in the best interests both of the Countess and of the island. He died very bravely, refusing the offer to be blindfolded. It is generally believed that all but one of the firing squad deliberately fired into the air.

The appeal to the King was upheld, though it came too late to save his life. His name was cleared and his estates were restored to his family. The other ringleaders of the rebellion against the Countess who had been imprisoned were released and their lands also restored to them.

William Christian has become one of the island's national heroes, and there is a well-known ballad *Baase Illian Dhone*, in which his life and deeds are commemorated. This story of William Christian and the Countess is one of the most exciting, mysterious and romantic of all the island stories.

Only two more Earls of Derby became Lords of Mann. They were followed by two Dukes of Atholl, and in 1765 the Lordship was sold to the British Crown who have held it ever since.

On the edge of Castletown harbour we saw the oldest building still in use in the island. Considerably older than Castle Rushen in its present form, it was used as a school continuously from the Middle Ages up to 1930, and housed the Castletown Grammar School. Now it is the headquarters of the local Boy Scouts. The building was erected as a Chapel about 1230 by the Cistercian monks of Rushen Abbey and dedicated to St. Mary, patroness of the Order. Gothic arches and roof timbers and panelling added in medieval times vouch for its antiquity.

Apparently the chapel survived the dissolution of the monastic establishments by Henry VIII and continued to be used as the church of Castletown for 150 years after. The Grammar School is likely to have grown from a school established there even before the Reformation. It was established on a regular basis by Bishop Barrow in 1665. He also founded the Academic School from which King William's College grew, although the idea of this latter

Elphin Glen
with view of Ramsey

Guthrie's Memorial, T.T. Course, near Ramsey

foundation appears to have come from the Great Earl of Derby who envisaged a 'Manks University'. Both schools carried on for many years under the roof of St. Mary's Chapel. The Grammar School continued to flourish even after 1830 when the Academic School was merged into the foundation of King William's College and I was told that many of the island's leading citizens had part of their education within its venerable walls.

Castletown, which was the old capital of the island, naturally teems with history and legend, as we continued to discover.

We had a peep at the picturesque old mansion across the harbour from the Castle which was once the official residence of the island's Governors. Now it is a holiday home. There is a christening font in the garden, probably dating from the tenth century. It came from an old chapel which once stood in the grounds. The graceful old-world garden and some picturesque masonry are attractive.

The two-hundred-years-old building alongside housed Quayles Bank—one of the first banks in the island. It was run by one George Quayle. The notes he issued were considered 'as good as the Bank of England', but his bank only lasted fifteen years, until 1817. Private banking was a hazardous business when Napoleon Bonaparte was raging his way across Europe and rumours caused frequent runs on the Banks' resources. George Quayle was a mechanical genius and, when the vault beneath the Bank was investigated by officials of the Manx Museum one hundred and forty years after it was closed, it was found to be fitted with an ingenious device of ropes and pulleys which acted as a kind of Heath Robinson burglar trap. Not only would any unauthorised person who entered be imprisoned but the room would be flooded by the tide. This vault was discovered during the war when R.A.F. men billeted in the upper part of the building found a hidden staircase behind the panelling. Happily for the Museum officials the ropes of the burglar trap had rotted and the pulleys were clogged with rust when they entered. They found thousands of bank notes which had never been issued, and dies and moulds for making coins.

Up to about sixty years ago Castletown was garrisoned by the only military force in the island—soldiers with scarlet tunics and pipe-clayed belts. The Barracks still stand in the market square, the one open space in the centre of the town.

Time has stood still in Castletown and the narrow streets present a headache for the local authority. Buses have had to be diverted from the centre of the town to miss the streets which were built for less sizeable traffic. Now they stop at the Brewery, which is on the Douglas side of the harbour. The houses crowd round the Castle as if they still looked to it for protection.

In the centre of the Market Place is a huge granite pillar which I thought should have a monument on it. Apparently I was right. In the early part of the nineteenth century the local folk decided to honour the Lieutenant-Governor, Cornelius Smelt, with a monument. But by the time the pedestal for the statue was erected the public subscriptions ran out.

We drove on, outside the town, to a most exciting converted stone barn run as a restaurant by Mr. Williamson, and known as 'The Witches' Kitchen'. After a tea of raspberries he took us up to the loft where he combines his profession as restaurateur with that of museum curator. I was immediately astonished at the wealth of his collection and the thoroughness of his lay-out.

I am not an authority on witch-craft or Cabalistic ritual but I was quite entranced by what I saw.

His display is set out behind glass in the most expert fashion and is in three sections. One part is enclosed by a glass and wooden partition which cuts off the whole of one end of the loft.

This has been made into a colourful temple with a rectangular central altar, an ornate bronze incense holder, several altars of fire, water, earth and sky, standing in the middle of a nine-foot concentric circle of three differently coloured rings.

Colour, Mr. Williamson assured me, plays a tremendous part in this worship. Psychic (is that the word?) power is generated and evoked in this circle, and I can well believe that at night it is easy to feel the occult influence.

I couldn't understand the nature of the various wands of office that lay round the circle. Night and day, light and darkness, are powerful factors in this worship. So is mathematics, and Mr. Williamson quoted at length from the work of Dr. John Dee (born at Southwick) who was both an eminent mathematician and astrologer at the court of Queen Elizabeth, whose horoscope he foretold with extreme accuracy when she was still a prisoner in the Tower of London.

At the end of the loft was a much smaller witches' circle with a dark lead treasure chest which used to hold coins. It was easier to evoke spiritual influences in a small circle because the power would be more concentrated in a small space. This circle was much darker than the other.

In cases round the walls were some horrific pictures of Mau-Mau tortures, showing the influence of black magic on the African natives. Here were examples of vengeance and cruelty in their most ruthless forms. I particularly noticed the dried banana skin slots into which blood was poured and over which the Mau-Mau oath was taken.

There was a history of the whole Mau-Mau movement which made very unpleasant reading.

The rest of the exhibition contained curious rings and jewels, images of whole bodies and of genitals stuck with pins, coins of gold and silver inscribed with numerals and cabalistic signs, models of a black cat, pictures of a witch Margaret and her son being burnt at the stake at Castletown, phallic symbols, and all sorts of charms, including the bollen bone that all Manx sailors carry, a model of the hammer of Thor.

Everything, said Mr. Williamson, in witchcraft has to be made by hand and everything is designed to beat down bodily resistance to the supernatural powers.

Here I saw the symbols that were the forerunners of designs used by the Rosicrucians and Freemasons, pentacles and talismen, the curious wand, a sort of divining rod, used by Matthew Hipkins, the famous witch hunter, the curved knives used for cutting herbs, usually sickle-shaped to show the influence of the moon, love charms and philtres, hideous masks, rings made from human bones, a Tibetan rosary of bones and instruments used to whiten (white plays a most important part in witchcraft) and many of the charms still used in the island to cure diseases of cattle and men.

I learnt that the Manxmen were always averse to the shedding of blood and that there were only two instances of witches being burnt at the stake.

I should have liked to have discovered the reaction of some typical Lancashire trippers to this exhibition, but I was not surprised to hear that, though the majority come to scoff, they are usually very much impressed by what they see, as indeed I was.

This is a very comprehensive exhibition but Mr. Williamson never made it clear whether he himself believed in its authenticity or was merely a detached observer of a most curious phenomenon in human nature.

As he said, something that has lasted seven thousand years must have something in it. His work, somewhat naturally, has aroused suspicion and even hostility among certain sections of the islanders—he admitted cheerfully that he is blamed for almost anything untoward that happens in the neighbourhood. But it is quite impossible to see this exhibition and remain unmoved. Here is something uncanny, a dabbling in the supernatural which may induce a wholesome dread of the unknown, but is at any rate scientifically of sufficient importance to warrant the kind of serious research that Mr. Williamson is devoting to it. It is obviously a costly business and is a whole-time job.

One of the most interesting things about it, in Mr. Williamson's view, is tracing the relative interest in the cases by noticing the amount of handsmears left on the glass after the clients have gone.

Mau-Mau has, of course, the greatest topical interest, and the crowd like pictures. Their interest in the coins and symbols is less acute.

It is by far the most comprehensive collection of witches' relics that I have seen. The only comparable collection is that in the Folk Museum at York, and that comes a long way behind it.

I was surprised to learn that one of the richest areas in which we find these relics is Sussex, which I have always regarded as one of the least superstitious regions in the British Isles.

On the way to Port St. Mary the old mansion house of Balladoole was pointed out to me. It is the ancestral home of the diplomat, Sir Ralph Stevenson. Six generations of his family held Balladoole before 1511. They are probably the oldest known landed family in the island. The old records show that Reginald Stevenson of Balladoole was a member of the House of Keys in 1417, and there was a Stevenson in the Keys from that time continuously up to 1897.

The house is the old square-face type standing in rich cultivated farmland.

On the estate a few hundred yards from the house is a Viking burial ground. Many relics were found when the site was excavated some years ago. I thought it was remarkable that so many of these ancient graves had been found intact in recent years, and discovered that it is partly due to the superstitious nature of the Manx people. It seems that superstitious fear prevented the farmers from disturbing the graves because they believed death and plague would come to the farm animals if they did so.

Topping a rise in the road from Balladoole, a marvellous vista was opened out of miles of coast line with Port St. Mary and the great rock of Bradda Head in the background. In contrast to the rocky cliffs around Douglas, here was a gentle shelving shore with the waves lapping against the coast-road at high tide.

Another old family house, Kentraugh, was surrounded by a thick mass of trees. They are the only trees in the vicinity and stand out for miles.

I was surprised to find how self-contained these old mansions were. This one once had its own brewery and the owner also kept a private bank. Both these buildings are near the house. There is also an example of an old-time ice box, a concrete structure like an army pill-box built into the ground. When in use, it was packed with ice taken from a pond, and this helped to keep meat and other food in good condition for a long time.

I noticed an inscription over the gate :

"Judge not your fellow-man's condition,
"Until you be in his position".

Philosophy which struck me as sound. An iron rod across the entrance to the drive automatically opened the gates when a carriage passed over it.

I was told that at one time there were thirty-seven breweries in the island. It is still well served in the art of beer-producing.

Port St. Mary has a picturesque harbour, good sands, a small promenade and a large yellow hotel called Balqueen Hydro. One outstanding feature of the place is that the Lifeboat is always kept afloat. It is the haven where all the small sailing boats are kept.

The headquarters of the Isle of Man Yacht Club are at Port St. Mary, and most of the boats in the harbour belong to members of the club. Many of them built the boats themselves. Evidently they have inherited some of the skill in boat building from their ancestors. Fishing boats and small schooners were built at Port St. Mary and Castletown at one time. About seventy years ago Port St. Mary was a thriving fishing village with one hundred and fifty boats registered there. The schooners were used to export the barrels of salted herring. Some of them went as far as the Baltic with it.

Now it is the favourite resort for amateur fishermen. I saw a lot of them on the breakwater.

I noticed also a big yachting pool which, I was told, was constructed by local model yachting enthusiasts. They have evidently got ships of one kind or another in their blood in this village.

It is a higgledy-piggledy sort of place with old cottages and villas dotted without plan or pattern in every corner of the cove. There is a golf course at the back of the town. Nearby is the enclosed cove of Perwick.

We drove up the hill and gained the high land of the Mull Peninsula, the southernmost part of the main island, our destination being the village of Cregneish, the oldest Manx village and a stronghold of Manx tradition, which overlooks the narrow strait which separates the main island from the Calf of Man.

My escort, who was in adventurous mood, turned suddenly to the left down a narrow lane.

"I think this is the road for the Chasms," he remarked,

"I haven't visited them for twenty years, so I can't be certain."

The road was narrow.

"I hope you'll be able to turn the car," I remarked.

I had visions of facing a chasm and being unable to turn back.

"Sure," he said, "They had a place selling pop there when I was a boy and I don't suppose they carried the bottles all this way."

It was all right. We reached, first an R.A.F. Establishment, then a small plateau of green grass, which was obviously a car park. When we got out and looked over the far wall at the magnificent coast panorama that lay in front of us, there was no doubt—at the bottom of the long, steep slope of rough grass in front of us there was a white-washed house with THE CHASMS painted in large letters on its wall.

We started to descend. I was glad I was not carrying a couple of dozen bottles of ginger pop. Indeed, the guardians of The Chasms must have got weary of pop-carrying themselves through the years, as the only commodities that were advertised for sale at the house were milk and eggs, doubtless home-produced.

We now paid the entirely reasonable sum of 2d. each to view one of the most unusual natural phenomena that I have seen. The cliffs at this point have been split, either as a result of a landslide or earthquake, from top to bottom by a series of rifts which form deep crevasses. In traversing these, except at a number of carefully chosen places, one risks a fall of several hundred feet.

We were still, of course, several hundred feet above the sea, even at the cliff's edge and, immediately below us, we could see the waves dashing against the base of Sugar Loaf Rock, which lay immediately off the small headland to our left. This coast scenery reminded me of Sark or

Cornwall at its grandest. With the heather and low gorse bushes around us, it gave the Isle of Man a picturesque quality that I have seldom seen in my many years of travel.

The promontory along the coast to the southwards was, I was told, Spanish Head, the south-westerly extremity of the island where, according to tradition, one of the galleons of the Spanish Armada was wrecked.

We returned to the car and continued our journey the short way to Cregneish. Here, we inspected the Folk Museum which occupies Harry Kelly's cottage, a one-storeyed, white-washed, thatched 'black' house type with open hearth, earth floor, Welsh dresser, glazed earthenware, grandfather clock, roof lined with peat, fishermen's net, peat cutting tools, and a double bed in the second room. Nearby is the handloom shed and in a third cottage are carpenter's tools, sheep shears and other instruments, the whole being arranged to show that a crofter's livelihood depended partly on the sea, partly on cultivating his garden, partly on weaving his own clothes and partly on digging his own fuel.

A little further down we stood on the edge of the water that separates the main island from the Calf, and the swiftness of the current showed how difficult it would be to row over.

A large rock with seaweed, occupied by gulls, stood in mid-stream, so that there are really two straits to cross if you want to make a direct passage. On the further side I saw a grass track leading up to a barn. The farm lies behind the top of the hill.

I was told you could find white heather on the Calf of Man. It is a rugged little island of about 600 acres and the sole occupants are Mr. Fred Faragher, the warden for the National Trust, and his wife. In the summer it is a little paradise of nature, but in the winter Mr. and Mrs. Faragher are sometimes isolated for considerable periods by the weather.   Thousands of birds, some of them rare, nest on the island, and seals bask in the creeks on the south side. There are also wild goats and innumerable rabbits.

There are about 150 acres of cultivated land around the farm and the farm house, which is the only habitable building on the island. It was built in 1878 by one of the 'Kings' —former owners—of the Calf. It has eleven rooms, a hot and cold water system—the water coming from a small private reservoir—and is wired for electric light, the current being generated by a small plant.

A Latin inscription above the door of the farmhouse calls it 'the little house in the great peace'.

In clear weather, England, Scotland, Wales, Ireland and, of course, the Isle of Man can be seen from its three hundred feet high cliffs.

The National Trust acquired the island in 1930, when it was purchased from a Yorkshireman, Mr. J. A. Popplewell, anonymously, and handed over to the Trust.

Most notable of the 'Kings' of the Calf was a London barrister named George Carey who gave up a career to live there. He brought a staff of retainers with him and developed the island and revelled in the open air life. He was reputed to have said, "I would rather live on the Calf in my lifetime than go to heaven when I die."

There was even a public house there then.

I saw boats bringing visitors to the Calf from Port St. Mary and Port Erin.   On these trips they must see some of the grandest coast scenery in Britain.

Two lighthouses were built on the Calf, but are now in disuse, their functions being performed by the Chicken Rock Light off the coast. There is also the remains of an old house which I could see from the mainland. I was told it was known as 'Bushel's House'. It is supposed to have been erected by a man named Bushel who lived in the reign of Queen Elizabeth. He murdered a lady in a fit of jealousy and escaped from justice by living in the seclusion of the Calf of Man.

The Calf also has on it the remains of a Viking lookout post and the foundations of an ancient chapel, in which was found a rare cross over 1000 years old.

I was right about the current in the Sound which separates the Calf from the mainland. In places the tide runs at eight knots and is impassable. Many ships have been wrecked in the vicinity. It was the scene of a disaster in 1852 when the brig *Lily*, of Liverpool, was driven on Kitterland, the rock in the centre of the Sound. The crew were saved and when the weather calmed thirty men under orders from Lloyds went aboard to salvage the cargo. By some unknown cause, sixty tons of gunpowder, which formed part of the cargo, were ignited and blew up. Only one man of those working on or near the wreck escaped alive.

Kitterland was supposed to be named after a Norwegian baron named Kitter. The legend is that he was a great hunter and went to the Calf to hunt red deer which were said to roam there. While he was away his castle on South Barrule was set on fire by peasants who hated him and, seeing it burning, he and his followers hastily embarked to return to the mainland. But the weather was bad and the boat was driven on Kitterland rock and they were all drowned.

We saw a tremendous lot of sea traffic going up and down the Irish Sea and got a distant view of the Mountains of Mourne.

We drove on over the heather-covered headland to the Circle of Mull, which is a prehistoric burial ground of late Neolithic or early Bronze Age, consisting of a circle of cists in six pairs with passages between each pair.

This entailed a scramble over stunted gorse up to a war relic of look-out and gun emplacements, from which we looked down on the protected sandy cove of Port Erin, a very prosperous-looking resort, with a chain of fine hotels.

We drove down a very steep, rough lane to the town passing on the way the Manx artist, Mr. Hoggatt, who lives there.

There is a fine marine drive round the harbour, at the end of which stands an aquarium. On the top level above the sands is a street or promenade of hotels, and behind them is an extremely well-laid out golf course round a high rock. There are any number of white-washed houses dotted about the cliff side which ends at Bradda Head, on the top of which stands a curious tower built by Milner, of Milner's Safes, in the likeness of one of his safe keys.

There are more palm trees here than I have seen elsewhere in the Island, though I have been told that they are not indigenous to the Island.

On the way back to Douglas we saw Colby Glen. We approached it through a clump of high trees—unusually high for this part of the Island, where there are few trees and most of them not very big. At first the thick foliage made the glen seem dark and rather forbidding, but having passed through the thick shrubs, we found charming, sunny banks and a stream winding in a horse shoe through a series of rocky pools. There were a lot of small trout basking in the pools. The glen had a great deal of picturesque undergrowth, and in places the sides were steep with occasional outcrops of rock.

On leaving Colby village we noticed an old-fashioned square-faced house with a stone tablet over the door on which was engraved, "In this house built by himself lived and died Archibald Cregeen, compiler of the Manks Dictionary, Born 1774—died 1841." His dictionary of the Manx language was the first to be published and is the most authentic record of the language in existence. It took him thirty years to compile it and he incurred the wrath of his wife, who felt he was paying too much atten-tion to the dictionary for her enjoyment of life. The dictionary was a remarkable achievement for a man who was virtually self-educated.

Cregeen was also Coroner for the sheading of Rushen and featured in an important event in Manx history. In 1825, Bishop George Murray, a nephew of the Governor-in-Chief of the Island, the Duke of Atholl, attempted to levy a tax on potatoes grown by farmers and crofters, most of whom were already poverty-stricken and over-burdened with taxes. There were riots in various parts of the Island. An attempt was made to burn the Bishop's Palace. Although he was an officer of the Government, Cregeen sided with the people. He presented a petition to the Bishop, who eventually surrendered and withdrew the tax.

I don't know if tax-resisting has become a habit with the Manx but, as we know, Income Tax is lower than in Eng-land and the growing of potatoes is now subsidised by the Manx Government.

The land is flat from Colby down to the sea, which is about three miles away. We could see the train on the single track railway on the stretch between Castletown and Port St. Mary. On the land side of the village the hills rise steeply but there are some good farms on the slopes.

We passed Arbory Church where Quilliam, the steers-man of Nelson's *Victory*, lies buried. John Quilliam was a lieutenant in a frigate at the Battle of Copenhagen. The frigate came under heavy fire and all Quilliam's superior officers were killed so that he was left in command. When Nelson called out to enquire how he was getting on, Quilliam is supposed to have answered 'Middlin' ', for it is a curious thing that very many Manxmen will rarely say 'Good' or 'Bad'. It is invariably somewhere in be-tween—'Middling'. At Trafalgar, Quilliam was in the

Victory and steered the ship because the steering gear had been damaged and he had had to fix it himself.

The sole remaining parish fair held in the Island is held every June at Arbory. It is called *Laa Columb Killey* (Arbory Parochial Festival). Now it consists of a flower and vegetable show, a parade of school children, sports and sideshows but it has its origin in medieval times.

In the village of Ballabeg we saw a fourteenth-century Franciscan Friary Chapel which, I was told, was used for years as a farm building. It is believed to have been founded in 1373 by the then Lord of Mann, William Montacute, Earl of Salisbury, and to have been built by the same masons who rebuilt Castle Rushen after its destruction by Robert the Bruce. It was occupied by Franciscan friars brought from Ireland by the Lord of Mann, and served as a Friary up to the dissolution of the monasteries. It is the only monastic chapel in the Island with a roof on. It is of Gothic design and has Caernarvon arches on the door and windows similar to those in Castle Rushen.

Some years ago two stones were found on the site bearing inscriptions in Ogam, the ancient writing of the Druids, indicating that it was the scene of a pre-Christian place of worship.

The same masons are believed to have built Monks Bridge at Ballasalla, which is the oldest bridge in the Island.

We passed through Ballasalla, which also has a quaint humped-backed bridge and an old church. The River Silverburn flows through the village and cars drive through a ford in the river in one place where the road is continued only by a footbridge.

We followed a tree-shaded walk alongside the river to Silverdale, which has a small lake for boating, an old water wheel and some magnificent chestnut trees.

The river is shallow and, like most of the rivers in the

Island, has lots of small trout which dart about from the sunlit splashes of water into the shadows. They did not seem to be as trusting as those in Colby river. Silverdale has a café, swings and one of the finest roundabouts of hobby-horses I have seen. The roundabout is driven by a water wheel on a stream running from the lake. There were a lot of children about, but the paths further up were secluded.

*　　　*　　　*

During and after dinner we watched a sober, slow and enormous procession of fresh visitors landing from several ships and making the long trek to their buses and boarding houses. We then walked along the front and heard some noisy singing in the hotel bars and watched large numbers consuming fish and chips as they stood in groups in shop doorways. The rest of the visitors were either sitting out on the front, fishing from the promenade or dancing at the Villa Marina.

SATURDAY   *The Curragh—Sulby Glen—Onchan*
                          —Niarbyl Cove—Dalby—Glen Maye

It was very much warmer when I got up this morning. Instead of getting up at four o'clock as I usually do, I was woken by the hoot of an outgoing steamer at 6.30, and got out of bed to see an astonishing procession, or rather series of parallel processions of home-going visitors trekking along the piers to the steamers. They look exactly like ants, or alternatively, a vast football crowd queueing up before entering the ground.

They are extraordinarily orderly and quiet. Perhaps many of them are suffering from hang-overs from visits to saloon bars last night.

63

These processions go on hour after hour and give one some slight inkling of the popularity of the Island.

We were called for at ten o'clock and driven by way of the Baldwin Valley up the Glass River along a quite deserted road past a large reservoir below Injebreck. It is the existence of this reservoir which allows all the visitors in Douglas to use as much water as they like, even in a drought. The reservoir holds three hundred million gallons of water and was made in 1905. It is eighty feet deep and three hundred yards long. There are steep hills on three sides, two of them thickly wooded on the lower slopes. Right up on top of the hill on the north side we could see an isolated little church dedicated to St. Luke. It is a branch of Kirk Braddan Parish Church and was built in 1836 by Bishop Ward, who was noted for his building of churches. St. Luke's is on the site of a keeil over one thousand years old and built into the gable is a sixth-century Celtic cross.

About three hundred yards further up the hill (Carraghyn) we could see the Killabane mound, one of the old sites of the Tynwald parliamentary assembly. To reach it we walked a quarter of a mile on the Norsemen's mountain road, the Via Regia (The Royal Way), which went from Skyhill near Ramsey to Castle Rushen. Most of the way it has a rock base worn smooth by the primitive sleds of the ancient people.

The Killabane mound is on an exposed spot, but gives a marvellous view over the fertile Baldwin Valley right down to Douglas. The old Statute Book of the Island records a meeting of Tynwald there in 1429. A decision made at that Meeting was that 'all disputes shall be determined by God and the Country and not by Prowesse'. Up to then it seems that arguments were settled by combat.

Baldwin Fair, one of the old Manx fairs, which were held in most of the parishes, was held at Killabane up to 1834.

Port Erin.

Port St. Mary

The Baldwin Valley divides into two forks and above the eastern fork we could see the Deemster's Cairn above Arderry. It is a curious monument of white stones built into a mountain wall. The white stones form the shape of a man, and the traditional story associated with it is that a Deemster (High Court Judge) was riding over the mountain to Castle Rushen and lost his way in a fierce snowstorm and perished. The monument marks the spot.

Above the reservoir I saw two rocky ravines with boisterous streams running through them. It is wild country and very picturesque. There were a lot of rabbits about, but little other sign of animal life. They seemed less timid than most we had seen and showed no alarm at the approach of our car.

I noted examples of the old-fashioned forerunner of barbed wire in the construction of some of the hedges. It consisted of pointed stones stood on end in the sods of the hedges to prevent sheep from jumping over.

We then began to climb and I saw an enormous number of black-faced mountain sheep, some shorn, some still in their long shaggy fleece, some horned, all feeding on good grazing grass on the hill slopes which were brilliant with fresh purple heather. There were also Galloway cattle and one Hereford bull.

I was told that Mr. Drummond (of Drummond's Bank) has gone into partnership with the farmer on these hills in experimental breeding on the marginal land.

The scene reminded me of the Yorkshire dales. There were the same gated ways, the same dark gritstone walls succeeded by hedgeless roads on the top and much coarse grass. The land seemed dry and well drained. Snaefell to our right was shrouded in cloud but the rest of the Island was clear.

We drove over the top and came to the Sulby watershed and followed the tiny watercourse along the top of a narrow treeless ravine with frequent scars where the banks had fallen in. There was no sign of any house beyond one deserted shepherd's hut and there were no walkers or motorists. There was a bothie and a sheep-dipping station in the hollow below. I noticed a great amount of white stone everywhere, especially on the track going off to the one farm which is called Druidale.

Far to the north-east and north we caught sight of the hills of Dumfries and Galloway; we passed any number of old overgrown trackways. Then we descended to a valley and the slopes of the hill were scarred with neglected intakes now overgrown again with bracken. At the foot of the hill we called in at the Ravensdale Castle Hotel, which has a high square tower and is a converted country house with a swimming pool.

We drove on by way of a number of villages, all with white-washed cottages, past Ballaugh new church which has a tall steeple, to Ballaugh old church, which has huge white leaning pillars as gate-posts and a fine white porch. Beyond it lay the handsome rectory and Walpole Farm, which is an attractive-looking guest house.

We saw the place where Professor Edward Forbes lived as a boy. He was a famous naturalist and scientist in the middle of the last century. He held a chair in Geology at Edinburgh University and was President of the Geological Society. He was also a poet and an artist. Before he was ten years old, he was said to have had a museum of natural history of his own, to which a wing of his father's house was devoted.

A rough track led down to Ballaugh beach but it looked little used.

We passed a field of little haycocks, each with an air hole at the bottom, and so came to the sea at a deserted place, where I saw a vast stretch of sands and sand-dunes and red sandy cliffs, but not a soul about except one family. We could see south as far as Peel cliffs and north to crumbling cliffs, which showed how severe is the coast erosion here.

We drove on by way of a maze of small lanes to cross the Curragh, a lost mere or marsh, by way of an overgrown track. It was like forging our way through the virgin jungle. The land on either side was filled with dense thickets and there were frequent dykes running off at right angles to the track. There had been attempts to grow flax which had failed, but we saw the flax grown wild. It reminded me of Wicken Fen, the National Trust insect, bird and rare plant sanctuary near Cambridge. There is a movement to turn the Curragh into a similar sanctuary. It is certainly a very exciting, exotic and totally unexpected piece of country that I should never have discovered without a guide.

The area was a paradise of bird life. I saw water fowl which I had not seen anywhere else. The bog is spreading and the Manx Government has a scheme under consideration to drain it. Many acres of good farmland are gradually going under water from the Curragh. It is in a saucer of land which makes drainage difficult. Two wide trenches which were cut many years ago in an attempt to get the water away are largely bound up with grass and weed, but next spring it is proposed to clean and improve them. Engineers who have studied the problem estimate the cost of a complete drainage scheme at £26,000. The roads through the Curragh run between the bogs and ponds. They are sound and safe but the surface is not good for motor vehicles. There are many rare plants growing there. It is sheltered and hot in the summer.

Curragh in the Isle of Man is pronounced Currack. I saw a great deal of cotton grass everywhere, sure sign of a spongy morass and bog.

After several miles we came again to a road at a level crossing and then climbed up Sulby Glen by way of an attractive common, along the side of the river and then across it near the place where the old bridge had been swept away in 1932.

We saw a farm alongside the Claddagh common which was owned by a man named Bacon who was something of a humorist. Because his name was Bacon, he incorporated a pig in the family crest. The crest is carved in the wall of the old farmhouse.

Sulby Glen is known as the Island's Little Switzerland. The glen is about half a mile wide with steep hills and cliffs on either side. In the lower part of the glen the Sulby river, alongside which the road runs, is wide and anglers say it is a good spot for fly-fishing. The river forms a series of deep pools higher up which are said to have plenty of trout in them.

On our right there was one of the most unusual farms I have seen. The farmhouse is down in the glen near the road, but the farmer has an almost vertical climb of four hundred feet up to the fields he farms, which are on top of a kind of small plateau.

Looking down to the river there is a quaint stone bridge which is one of the oldest in the Island. The track which once passed over it led to the upland farms which have now all vanished.

After passing a woollen mill we climbed again to the bare mountain and I had to open more yellow gates. I saw a pleasant little glen called Tholt-y-Will running off the main glen. Just at the top we passed three long barrows which still await excavation.

Three of the Island's seventeen parishes join near Tholt-y-Will. These are Michael, Lezayre and Braddan, which adjoins Douglas but sends a long neck northwards to this point. They say, "If you had three legs you could put a foot in each of them".

There are more trees in this part than anywhere else in

the Island. The hills all round are thickly planted with firs, and in one place different varieties have been used to get a chess-board effect, which looks very spectacular from the opposite side of the valley. It is these trees that give the area its Swiss appearance.

Tholt-y-Will glen is also thickly wooded. The turbulent stream which runs through it breaks into waterfalls in several places and I noticed that the paths which had been made through the glen gave excellent clear views. If there are any squirrels in the Island it is here I would expect to see them. But we did not see any.

We made the steepest ascent I have struck, climbing out of the glen to Snaefell. The heather was brilliant on the hills round here. It is remarkable how many different shades of red, pink and purple there are.

The road cuts through a gap in the Great Wall, a mile-long fortification running over the mountain side built about Roman times, by whom and for what particular purpose is obscure, but it is clearly defined. It is a big earth and stone structure about fifteen feet thick at the base.

Close to a large peat-cutting section of the moor we turned again through a gate to a narrow overgrown track which led us down over a moor of black-faced sheep to Glen Roy, which reminded me of the Derbyshire moors near Ashover. I was told that there were grouse but that they were nearly all poached, so they were not worth preserving.

One thing I particularly like about these gated roads is that the notice on them doesn't read 'Private' but 'Please shut gate. Penalty £2'.

It is particularly important at the T.T. race period to keep the sheep which graze on the mountains from straying on to the roads over which the races pass. Some of them have a system of grids alongside the gates over which traffic can pass but over which sheep will not go. I believe this idea was devised by an old Manxman named Thomas

Stowell who lives at Glen Roy. He is also in charge of the peat-cutting concessions on the Beinn-y-Phott (Peat Mountain). I was told there is a tremendous depth of peat there, but I noticed there are not many claims.

If anyone wants to work one, all they have to do is to apply to Mr. Stowell who allocates an area. Mr. Stowell himself remembers when carts from all the farms in the surrounding districts went up to Beinn-y-Phott to get peat which had been cut in the spring. They could cut enough in a week to provide the farm with fuel for the whole year.

From the road I was able to see right down through the glen to the sea, as well as, of course, the electric trams winding round the sides of Snaefell. The track which runs from Laxey crosses the main mountain road from Ramsey. We joined this at the Bungalow, an inn which is one of the favourite vantage points for spectators of the motor cycle races.

We were soon in Onchan, where we visited the open-air Grotto of our Lady of Lourdes. Here there were benches, an image of the Virgin, an altar, candles and an artificial grotto made of concrete. Non-Catholics are invited to the services which are held at 10.30 and 4 o'clock on Sundays. There is also a new cycle track and about a dozen hard tennis courts. Onchan has its own beach, Port Jack, but it joins Douglas much as Hove joins Brighton.

Against the wall of Onchan Parish Church I saw an old whipping post. In the church there is a drawing of a cock on the chancel wall. The artist, Henry Corbould, R.A., was art master to the children of Queen Victoria, and was a frequent visitor to the Island in the middle of the nineteenth century. The story is that he was visiting the Vicar of Onchan and burned a stick in the fire to draw the cock with the charcoal in view of its association with St. Peter to whom the church is dedicated.

Corbould also had the idea of creating a statue of King Orry the Dane, first of the great Norse Kings of Mann, as an exemplification of the greatness of the golden age in Manx history. He made drawings and interviewed several influential people, including the Prince Consort, who visited the Island in 1847, but owing to the lack of local co-operation the scheme did not mature.

An unusual stone in a field alongside the church was said to be sacred. A story is that the wife of one of the vicars was irritated because it partly blocked the path through the churchyard. One day she pushed it over the wall of the churchyard on to unhallowed ground of the adjoining meadow. That night she was struck dead by lightning while lying in bed beside her husband. He was unhurt. The villagers said it was retribution for her interference with the sacred stone.

We saw the old Hague farmhouse on the side of Summerhill Road where Captain Bligh of the *Bounty* had his honeymoon. Bligh came to the Island to visit a friend, William Betham, who was the first collector of customs for the British Government after the Duke of Atholl sold the customs rights of the Island. He married Betham's daughter, Mary. By a strange coincidence Fletcher Christian, who led the *Bounty* mutineers, was a member of a family who lived in the north of the Island, and Peter Heywood, a midshipman in the ship, was the son of a Deemster. Three separate connections with the *Bounty*, all from the Isle of Man, are very odd.

Part of the Hague farmhouse is over two hundred years old. It has the old type of farmhouse steps up the side of the building. There is a well in the farmyard.

The Douglas Corporation has made an attractive glen available to the public in this vicinity. The entrance is at the bottom of Summerhill and we walked through tree-shaded paths with the inevitable bubbling stream that runs alongside up to the Governor's Bridge. It seems to be the admirable principle of the islanders to make a glen out of every ravine.

After luncheon, we were taken by the old road to Castletown, a most attractive deserted way with many fine private houses lying back from the road in trees at the ends of long avenues. Most of the houses are yellow-washed and square.

The first mile of the road was entirely overhung by large trees and the sun glinting through made it a cathedral of nature. The variety of greens in the foliage was very attractive.

I noticed an old stone house which looked like a small church. I was told it was the first Catholic Church built in the Island. It was built through the agency of Lieutenant John Taubman of the Nunnery, who was an officer in a military unit called the Manx Fencibles. The Fencibles were sent to Ireland in 1798 at the time of the Irish Rebellion, and Lieutenant Taubman met and made friends with a priest who, six years later, turned up in the Isle of Man with the object of founding a Catholic mission. He met with some opposition, but his old friend Lieutenant Taubman befriended him and gave him a site near his home at the Nunnery. The Chapel was called St. Bridgid, to which Saint the Nunnery was dedicated.

We passed under a very solid-looking bridge over which the little trains of the Isle of Man Railway run. I was told the buses ran along this route until the first double-deckers arrived in 1946. Then they had to change the route because the buses were a foot too high to pass under this bridge.

I noticed several large fields of good oats just before we got to St. Marks. The farmers used to let their pigs roam on the sides of South Barrule. They became wild and were known as 'purrs' but all, or most of them, have been rounded up now.

In the valley below I noticed about a dozen roofless crofts, the homes of those who once worked the now derelict lead-mines.   Heather here grew in great profusion on the walls, whose stones contained a large amount of white quartz.

At the top of the hill we left the car to walk over the soft grass to peep over the edge of the high cliffs below the 'Hill of the Rising Sun'.   Fishermen used to make for port as soon as they saw the tip of the sun appear over the peak of this high sea cliff.

South Barrule, which lies inland, is known as the Hill of the Watch, and beacons used to be lit both on North and South Barrule, which could be seen from all over the Island.

Jill saw some herons flying over close to a cross roads known as the Round Table.   The sides of the mountain here are being planted with larch and spruce.

We descended to sea-level again at the Service Radar station at Dalby, and then got out at the delightful rocky cove of Niarbyl, which has two newly-thatched white cottages and a tea house that was closed.   This reminded me of Hartland Point owing to its rugged rocks.   Not much of a bathing place, but grand for scrambling about on the rocks.

We got a superb view of the cliffs as far as the Calf of Man.   Niarbyl, by the way, means Long Nose.

At Bellelby farm we saw standing against a barn door a stone cross which I was told had a remarkable history. It is about seven feet high and two feet wide.   The design of the cross is rare, being formed by a series of squares joined together.

It was brought there from an early Celtic Chapel called Keeill-y-Chiarn (Chapel of the Lord) which fell into ruins and is now ploughed over.

It seems that the Bellelby farm was connected with the

Northern Ireland monastery of Bangor and Saul. In 1204, John de Courcy, Lord of Ulster, married Aufrica, sister of King Reginald of Mann. She had a bad crossing from the Isle of Man to Ireland and vowed she would do something for the Church by way of thanks for her deliverance. Accordingly, she persuaded her brother to grant to the Barony of Bangor and Saul the rents of six farms in the Isle of Man, one of which was Bellelby. Presumably, the cross was placed in the old chapel by the Monks of the Irish Monastery.

We passed through Dalby where a noted Manxman named William Cashen was born in 1838. Cashen led a march of fifteen hundred fishermen on the Tynwald assembly at St. Johns in protest against the imposition by Lieutenant-Governor Loch of harbour dues on fishing boats. This was in 1874 and up to that time all fishing boats had been free from charges for the use of harbours, and the fishermen considered it a hereditary right. Fishing and farming were the staple industries of the Island and the fishermen from Peel and Port St. Mary represented a considerable force.

Governor Loch called out the military garrison at Castletown and they prepared to attack the demonstrators. But Cashen dispersed his forces and the affair seems to have been settled peaceably But the incident had its effect. The Governor had seen the power of the fishermen and later visited Peel and discussed the point at issue with Cashen. He eventually withdrew the dues.

Cashen also headed a strike of fishermen who demanded higher pay than nine shillings a week for overhauling and repairing nets in the winter. He was a broad-shouldered Viking, over six feet tall, with a great square beard. He sailed the world in small schooners and was shipwrecked in one of them only a few miles from his home. Cashen, in his day, spoke the Manx language fluently and headed a movement to continue its use. He strikes me as a typical Manxman in his love of the sea and his readiness to fight for his rights. These seem to be two characteristics that are to be found in all Manxmen right through the ages.

We drove up to 'West Wood' to have tea with ninety-year-old Mrs. Clegg, who instantly remembered our last visit with Vernon Bartlett seventeen years ago. She was delighted to see us. The tea room was hung with Millais prints.

We went on by way of Glen Maye and Glen Rushen, and once more took a rough, very narrow, overgrown track to the moor top, where we saw the chimneys of lead-mines known as 'Snuff the Wind'. The road was far too bad for any car, but our driver decided to try a track that he had never used, with the result that he came to a complete standstill, and had to back about half a mile. It was only with difficulty that we regained the track that took us down again to Glen Maye by way of a very steep, rough and winding lane. Glen Maye seen from above is a cluster of white cottages with slate roofs. The glen itself is another of the familiar tree-shaded dells, but with the difference that it breaks into a spectacular gorge as it nears the sea. There is a beautiful waterfall in it and the vegetation is thick. The original spelling was Glen Meay, which means 'Vale of Luxuriance'. There is a good sandy shore at the bottom of the glen. I discovered some fine caves on the north side, but I imagine they would be inaccessible when the tide is up. It is an ideal cove for bathers.

I had noticed a number of pinfolds, used to pen animals which strayed from the farms. Each parish had one. There was an excellent example at Patrick.

On the Patrick parish church wall I saw a sundial. The gnomon was supported by a metal Three Legs of Man. In the church there is a granite font presented, in 1714, by the greatest of Manx Bishops, Dr. Wilson, the scholar who did more than any other single man to restore the Manx tongue with his translation of the Bible and Prayer Book.

A big house nearby had two great stone ornaments at the main gate which looked like giant acorns. I was told they were pineapples and were put there by a former owner of the estate, named George Moore who was a prominent local figure two hundred years ago. He brought them to the Island from Bath. Moore was elected Speaker of the House of Keys and knighted.

We passed the nurseries of the Isle of Man Forestry Board. It is a very active body carrying out considerable tree planting each year. Lately they have planted large sections in Glen Rushen and South Barrule.

I noticed that a bridge carrying a railway line passed over the road near here. I was told it was the old line from St. Johns to Foxdale which was built when Foxdale mines were thriving. It finally went out of use with the coming of the buses.

At Crosby I saw Eyreton Castle, a monument to a disappointed man. It has an imposing entrance off the main road. The castle was built by a man named Eyre about a hundred years ago; although money and thought were obviously lavished on it, Eyre's dream was never to become a reality for money ran out and it was not completed. The castle stands in an idyllic setting of woods and mossy banks. There were hundreds of rooks in the trees although, rather curiously, I could see no sign of nests. I was told the birds congregate there in great numbers but do not nest there. They made a great clatter.

Between Crosby and Union Mills we turned off the main road at Ballafreer. The first roots of Christianity were supposed to have been planted here by St. Patrick when he landed at the Island in 444 A.D. With St. German he established a church at Ballafreer. The site of the church and the font are still there.

A feature of the old-world garden on the farm is the intertwining of two big yew trees which form seats known as 'The Courting Chairs'. These trees are referred to as 'old' in a book written one hundred and twenty-eight years ago.

We also saw The White Lady of Ballafreer, a peculiar rock of white quartz which has a human look about it. It is about seven feet high and is reputed to bring good fortune to young brides. The Island abounds with this mixture of history and legend. Most of the stories have been handed down by oral tradition and it is difficult to find any record of them in print.

Several of the people whom I had met today could speak a little of the Manx language but the native Manx speakers are very few now. One is a man living at the Curragh who is 100 years old. As an example of the Celtic strain in the language, I was quoted one of the many Manx proverbs : *"Myr sloo yn cheshagt share yn ayrn"*, which means "The smaller the company the bigger the share".

SUNDAY *Kirk Braddan—Maughold*

They talk much about the cruel sea, but it has struck me for the first time over here, where it has been so consistently windy that I have christened it 'The Windy Island', that the sea would never be cruel if it was not for the wind. Usually playful, she can suddenly and unaccountably lose her temper and become one with the Eumenides.

The foghorn sounded in the early hours but did not disturb me much. The glass has fallen considerably but, to my surprise, the day remained sunny with a high wind dispersing the clouds early. At 10.20 we set out by way of an attractive footpath running outside the Nunnery walls, the Power Station and a new housing estate, to attend the open air service at Kirk Braddan.

The road-side was lined with motor-coaches, well over a hundred of them, which had brought thousands of visitors to the steep hillside. There were ice-cream stalls outside and a large number of the congregation sat on the grass reading the Sunday papers. Others stood up and joined (rather feebly, I thought) in the hymns. Here seemed to me a golden opportunity for a modern Sermon on the Mount. But as the preacher dwelt, to my great surprise, on the grimness of life, in a resoundingly clear voice, nobody seemed to be listening very attentively. Milton's phrase of 'Blind Mouths' seemed to be applicable here. They all looked a little bewildered and uncomfortable. I felt that the congregation had come for the fivepenny ride and because it was a well-publicised occasion. It was rather like a football crowd without any match to stir the crowd's excitement.

These open-air services are popular in other parishes all over the Island. I believe that the Islanders enter into the true spirit of them more readily than do the visitors. At the foot of the hill stands the brick and stone new church, rather bare inside, where we found another morning service going on with a congregation of about a hundred. We stayed for Communion with perhaps fifty others.

It seems that the open-air service at Kirk Braddan started when the Reverend William Drury, the Vicar in 1856, held a Service in the churchyard because there was accommodation for no more than two hundred in the church. Since then, as many as 35,000 people have attended a single Service, and a total of over a quarter of a million people attend during the Summer. It strikes me as an admirable idea, but one that needs developing with immense care and tact if it is to have the desired effect of increasing true worship.   Above everything, it must not be allowed to degenerate into a picnic outing.

We took the bus home and passed a number of the open-air congregation who were walking home along the road.

We went up to the hotel bar.   No drinks are permitted on Sundays in the Island except to hotel residents.   Visitors in the hotels are not allowed to give drinks even to guests on Good Friday or Christmas Day, which seems a little harsh.

No steamer is allowed to sail between midnight on Saturday and midnight on Sunday, and an inevitable air of deadness hangs over the town.

After luncheon Mr. Cahn, the hotel manager, and his father, drove us past the Douglas holiday camp, which has a fine flower garden and many tennis courts which were being well patronised, to call on Mr. Arthur Karran, who took us on with Mr. William Cubbon, the 88-year old author of *Island Heritage*, in a Rolls-Bentley to see King Orry's Grave, a burial ground that has been cut in two by a road.   Part lies hidden in a cottage garden, part lies dangerously near a new housing estate.   It is only by a miracle that these prehistoric relics are preserved.

We then went by way of high-banked, narrow, overgrown lanes to a wonderfully situated prehistoric crematorium, or burial ground, triangular in shape, with the stones reddened by burning.

This hallowed place overlooks Maughold Point and lighthouse.   The only occupant was a black and orange butterfly, but we roused a mother partridge with three newly born chicks which had no idea of the power of the car and ran on so slowly down the middle of the lane that we had to stop and shoo them into the hedge.

On the other side of the burial ground, which dates back to 3000 B.C., I saw under stunted trees a white circular stone that marked the burial ground of the Quakers in 1676. I didn't realise that in the seventeenth century any interest was shown in prehistoric monuments, but they would scarcely have chosen that isolated spot by accident.

When we got back to the road I saw a signpost pointing towards the crematorium bearing the words 'Rullick-ny-Quakeryn', and 'Doarlish Allen'.

We drove across the deep gully to the village of Maughold where the fields are well cultivated, with good crops of oats and many sheep and beasts feeding.

The Manx sheep have four horns, golden eyes and brown wool, which is never dyed. There is also a species of Manx pony, short, shaggy like the Shetland, but both the sheep and ponies are in danger of extinction. The sheep we saw were white-faced and black-faced Suffolks.

Maughold was an Irish saint who was fettered and set adrift in a boat. He landed at this point, where a fisherman caught a cod, in whose stomach was found a key which unlocked the saint's fetters.

We passed the tiny cottage in which used to live the giant Kelly, the cast of whose hand we were later to see at Rushen Castle.

We passed also a herd of good-looking cows going back for the milking.

Maughold village stands round a small green with the churchyard, which contains an enormous number of brown stone tombstones standing above it. The most remarkable feature about it is the shed containing about twenty Celtic crosses and Ogham stones inscribed with runes. One stone contains an inscribed carving of a Viking ship, another the Manx chain ring, and a more elaborate one the story of Sigurd and Loki. One cross contains five balls which represent balls of wool or breasts. One is inscribed 'Crux Guriat'.

Near the tall grey column which commemorates Sir Hall Caine, C.H., K.B.E., the centenary of whose birth this

The Chasms with the Sugar Loaf Rock

A Cottage in Cregneish

year (1953) is also commemorated by a small urn, we came to the foundations of an ancient Keeill, floored with pebbles.

We saw the monument to Swinnerton, the Island sculptor, an example of whose work is to be seen in a very lifelike rope hung over one tombstone column. We saw, too, the grave of P. M. C. Kermode, the patriot archaeologist who devoted his life to unearthing the true facts about his Island's history, helped by his sister Josephine. Kermode was a Grand Knight of the Order of Falcons of Iceland, and lived from 1855 till 1932. His father was the local parson, who had seventeen children.

Another monument tells the main points in the life of Captain Hugh Crow, a slave trader who wrote a book to show that not everyone engaged in the trade was cruel and mercenary. I was told Crow was noted for his humane treatment of the blacks and they were named 'Jim Crows' after him. He believed they were better off working on Jamaican plantations than in their native Africa. Crow was famous for a fight with two French privateers in 1798, and an all-night battle he fought with two men-o'-war under the impression that they were Frenchmen. With the light of dawn he saw they were British. He retired to an estate in Maughold and became a Member of the House of Keys.

After tea in a cottage in the village, where we fed innumerable tame birds, we drove on past the lovely house 'Tranquillity', partly painted white and blue, the home of Mrs. Cunliffe-Owen, to the ancient church of St. Mary's, Ballure at the foot of the hill above Ramsey.

Here there is a holy well and a memorial to a Stowell (alias Brown) who died at the age of 44, leaving fifteen sons and one daughter.

"Each boy of this enormous family had a sister," said Mr. Cubbon, chuckling.

Several of the fifteen sons made names for themselves. One became the Attorney-General of the Island, another a famous clergyman, two were schoolmasters, another an artist and another a poet who wrote for the first Isle of Man newspaper, the *Manks Mercury*.

Mr. Cubbon also showed us a memorial to a joiner named Anderson. The tools of his trade are engraved on the stone—a saw, hammer, axe, square and dividers.

Ballure Church is the oldest building in Ramsey.

Mr. Cubbon showed us, as we climbed the mountain road of the T.T. course, the Via Regia that runs along the crest of Scaca or Sky Hill, the way by which the Norse invaders came after they landed in Scotland.

The Norsemen ruled the Island for two hundred years, from 1066, when Godred Crovan, who was the first Norse King, won the Island from the Celts. I saw the tree-dotted fertile banks on which the battle was fought. The story was preserved in the Chronicle of Man written in Latin by the monks of Rushen Abbey. Godred Crovan landed near Ramsey three times before he was successful. The third time he came by night and set an ambush of three hundred men in a wood at Scaca. During the heat of the battle the ambush was sprung in the rear of the defenders, and was the turning point of the fight. Godred's eldest son, Lagman, succeeded him, and then his second son, Olaf, who was crowned at the St. John's Tynwald.

Godred was a great warrior. He captured the Hebrides and raided Dublin and part of Leinster.

Glen Auldyn nearby is another of the picturesque ravines that are covered in ferns and trees, with a stream running through it. Following it up from Ramsey we could see it change into the treeless wildness of the mountains.

When we got back to sherry at Mr. Karran's house he showed us his delightful garden, from the edge of which he looks down on Douglas Bay, his cellars which the Navy used as a Radar station during the war, and many Manx books and relics.

I was most of all struck by an earthenware dish on which was painted a picture of his great-grandfather, Richard Karran, sitting at the tiller of a small sailing boat with dinghy, in Naples Bay below Vesuvius in 1797. He had sailed there from Port St. Mary single-handed at a time when the seas were infested by French privateers.

That was the best example of the Manx spirit that I have so far seen, but everywhere we met with legends and stories of great seamen.

Mr. Karran blew the ram's horn that was used as a fog-horn in olden days and showed us many other treasures which he had amassed.

The bay was crowded with small rowing boats as we drove home along the thronged front. There was an enormous queue for the Sunday concert at Villa Marina. On Sunday there is no dancing as well as no drinking, but people can row and they can listen to good music. After dinner, Mr. Drinkwater, the owner of the Scottie which spends all its meal-times facing the radiator away from the diners, kindly invited us back to his house one evening. He lives in the Island but is staying at the hotel while his house is being redecorated. He explained to us why so many English people have come over here to live. It isn't only for health's sake. There are no death duties, which is in itself a great inducement, and the Income Tax is about half what it is on the mainland.

MONDAY   *Port Erin*

Driving rain which obliterated sea and land greeted me as I looked out of the window at 6 a.m.

It was, we thought, obviously a morning for the Museum.

If archaeology is your hobby, the Isle of Man is the happiest of happy hunting grounds.

We never got to the Museum. We got along the front all right but when we tried the parallel shopping street, Strand Street, we found ourselves in the middle of a jostling, merry, singing crowd who seemed to be on their way in opposite directions to a Cup Final.

These Lancastrians adore company. They were all at their gayest and bumped each other like bumping cars in a fun-fair. In spite of the wind and rain, the men were, for the most part, bare-headed, and in their shirt sleeves. The girls wore plastic mackintoshes. I had not noticed before the prevalence of red-heads.

Two vans which attempted to make their way past the surging mob were greeted with loud cheers and only temporarily suspended the activities of a toy symphony orchestra which accompanied a band of singing boys in multi-coloured paper caps and their robust red-faced girl companions. I enjoyed the fun from the upper window of Lyons, a shop where we spent most of the morning trying to find a suitable mackintosh for Jill.

After trying several shops we found a 'Dannimac' at Lyons, that was smart and reversible, black on one side and bright green on the other. The cost was nine guineas and it looked much too good for scrambling through heather and brambles.

We then joined a melée in Woolworths. After this we needed refreshment and found it in the lounge of the Atholl, opposite the General Post Office, where several hundred visitors were busy sending postcards home.

We passed a well-filled bar called the 'Dog's Home', and I lamented the fact that we couldn't find a 'Kipper Bar', in view of the fact that almost every other shop advertised Manx kippers.

We saw a notice outside the Methodist Church advertising dancing in the Nunnery grounds under the auspices of the Church Council, which sounds progressive.

After luncheon we took the three o'clock bus to Port Erin. By virtue of sitting on the top deck we looked down on an amazingly colourful assortment of neat flower gardens.

The soil of the Island is particularly suitable for roses. Most of the larger houses have long drives and are almost entirely hidden by trees, obviously to protect them against the wind, which never seems to let up.

The journey takes about an hour, and passes through a number of small villages that have little architectural beauty, but all contain new housing estates of small neat houses, mainly white-washed.

We were enchanted by Port Erin, principally because it is so obviously a family resort, completely unsophisticated, with fine sands about half a mile long, in a deep inlet protected by a rocky breakwater from rough seas and the wind.

We were able to have our tea sitting out of doors in a white-washed cottage garden only separated from the beach by a low wall. We were served by a most attentive waitress, and had eggs and crab sandwiches as we watched families bathing, families playing cricket, families digging sand castles and families just lying about.

There were scores of small children and dogs chasing one another. Gradually, from across the sea, we saw the whole range of the Mountains of Mourne reveal themselves so clearly that they looked only a dozen miles or so away. In shape they looked very much like Capri seen from Naples.

A steep grassy bank separates the lowest tier of small lodging houses, each of which has a tiny rectangular patch of garden, from the grander hotels on the upper terrace. Down this bank children were continually rolling.

We walked round the southern arm of the bay after tea, and passed a shop full of crabs and scallop shells, an old, grey stone house of great antiquity where an ancient woman was taking in her washing, a red brick institute and a grey stone aquarium, Biological Station, and Fish Hatchery, before coming to some wild ragged rocks above a swirling, clear, blue and green sea.

Sea gulls were fiercely and neatly opening what looked like scallop shells and devouring the contents at one gulp.

The clouds which were massing up to the west miraculously missed us altogether and during the whole afternoon Port Erin remained bathed in sunshine.

There are a number of attractive secluded coves on the northern side of the bay under Milner's Tower, each reached by a narrow grass track from the top.

At the end of the harbour there is a broken down breakwater, but nearer in is a fine modern pier, under which were moored about a dozen motor yawls, each bearing the initials C.T., and some two dozen rowing boats. The breakwater, I was told, was built to make Port Erin a national harbour of refuge. It cost £70,000, partly Manx and partly English money. When the foundation stone was laid in 1864, Milner, of Milner's Safes, who was a great advocate of the development of the port, provided tubs of ale and a bullock to be roasted whole to celebrate the occasion. The breakwater was destroyed in a single night by a great storm which dislodged the fifteen-ton blocks of concrete. The blocks seemed to me to be firmly settled now and I was told that even the worst storms do not move them. It struck me that it would be a good idea to rebuild the breakwater With Bradda Head sheltering the other side I should think it would make the bay like a lake. There were a lot of young fishermen angling round the base of the ruined breakwater and also on the inner pier.

I was surprised to see how far out to sea the rowing boats went. Several of them seemed to be as much as three miles from the shore.

The motor boats ply between Port Erin and the Calf of Man and Port St. Mary.

We climbed up and round some steep ways to the back of the town and found an attractive sunken rock-garden, with a tiny stream, which was attracting a good number of children. Above, their elders were playing tennis or cultivating their gardens. One man was cutting thistles with a scythe.

Paths led from here to the top of Bradda Head, where a zig-zag path down the face of the cliff leads to the entrance to a disused copper and lead mine on the edge of the sea. I could see a wide band of white quartz in the rocky mass of the cliffs, which rise five hundred feet from the sea. Working these mines must have been a hazardous job. I was told they were the oldest workings in the Island. Lead and silver were mined there in the seventeenth century, and the mines were worked up to 1884. The ore was brought in boats to a smelting house at Port St. Mary.

On the way back to the station we saw St. Catherine's Well, which was formerly a holy well of a keeill. It was said that any woman who drank the waters was rejuvenated to a girl of 17. I imagine that the water must long ago have been drained away as I saw no queue.

The older part of Port Erin is down on the edge of the sea where the fishermen live. There are some excellent hotels and boarding houses on the upper promenade and we had a glimpse of an open-air swimming pool built into a creek on the north side. The banks of the creek form a natural amphitheatre.

The hills around Port Erin are striking. The village lies in a hollow between them. To the south are the Mull Hills, on the north side the western highlands and Cronk-ny-Irey-Lhaa, the fishermen's 'Hill of the Rising Sun'.

We found that the last train for the day left Port Erin at 5.35. I imagine that since the advent of the motor bus, the railway has become less well patronised.

We drank in the lounge of the Falcon's Nest Hotel,

which overlooks the oyster-shaped bay. We then caught the 6.40 bus and listened to a genial Lancashire family describing their boarding house experiences. So far as I could gather, they were sleeping about six to a room. Their main talk, however, ran on the exploits of their brilliant son who had taken, or was taking, his B.Sc., which apparently would qualify him for the position of Borough Surveyor.

We passed our usual flock of sheep and herd of cows. It is most curious that, in whatever direction we move, we seem to pass a single flock of sheep and a single small herd of cows. From this I ought to be able to form some estimate of the Island's wealth in sheep and cattle, but my only surmise is that there are about three times as many sheep as cattle.

We admired once more the spaciousness and lay-out of the Airport as we passed it on our return. We arrived back in time for dinner at eight, to watch the departure at 8.30 of a horde of passengers who left the harbour to resounding cheers and much hearty singing.

And so to work and early bed.

TUESDAY   *Garwick Glen—Ramsey—*
Bride—Jurby

It was cold, wet and windy as we waited in the bus queue from 9.55 till 10.15 for the Ramsey bus, and quite a crowd of men in open-necked shirts and girls in print frocks and no mackintoshes were waiting with us. I was not surprised at the sneezes and coughing. These Northerners are certainly hardy. They are incorrigibly cheerful and look well-fed, but they take no precautions at all against bad weather and today was thoroughly bad.

As usual at breakfast, I watched the mystery of the pier. Vast crowds collected to watch one of the ships go out.

Only later I learnt that this contained the Orangemen of Belfast who had been celebrating Orange Day (12th July) by a visit to the Isle of Man.

On the Ramsey journey we passed through Garwick, where I saw a mill wheel working, Lonan, which has an upstanding church and fine sea cliffs, and Laxey, where I had a better chance of looking down on the grey lead-mine workings, now, of course, derelict. This is in a deep ravine, with white houses clustering along the steep bracken-covered hillside.

Garwick Glen runs for about half a mile from the entrance on the main road to one of those secluded coves which we have discovered all round the coast. Garwick is undoubtedly one of the most attractive. The ferns and trees run almost down to the water's edge where there is a pebbly beach. A stream follows the course of the glen and runs out on the beach. The rocks on each side of the beach look as if it would be interesting to explore them. Garwick is said to be a haunt for mermaids. It is remarkable how the people have a story attached to almost every place in the Island. In this case it sounded possible. Garwick beach would provide an ideal setting for mermaids.

We saw the megalithic monument known as the Cloven Stones in Garwick. It is in the garden of a cottage. Instead of having the stones removed—which would have been a Herculean effort—the owner of the cottage built his garden wall round them. Tradition says that a Welsh prince was slain there during an invasion of the Island. Two of the great stones appear originally to have been one and to have been split by some unknown force.

Near the mill which I had seen working, there was a site of an ancient fort, probably of the Bronze Age. The Island is full of these historic remains, but I found surprisingly few people who seemed to be aware of them.

There was a good deal of fuchsia in the hedges and

hydrangeas among the sweet williams and roses in the cottage gardens.

The railway track, which runs alongside the road most of the way, is double here and single in the southern part of the Island.

Laxey has a fine stretch of sands and is very popular. Most of the farms we passed had fine herds of cattle, some Ayrshires, some mixed Guernseys and Jerseys, black-faced and white-faced sheep and usually geese and hens, but I saw only a few pigs.

Beyond Laxey are a number of stone quarries, some of slate, some of limestone, one of granite.

We passed at least three glens, the biggest of which were the Dhoon Glen and Glen Mona, all deep ravines entirely hidden by thick trees.

Most of the glens have waterfalls in them. None of them are very large but they are all fascinating. The most beautiful I found in Dhoon Glen. They are about half a mile from the sea and to reach them it is necessary to walk about that distance along the path hidden in the trees of the ravine. The variety of greens in the foliage is remarkable and the whole effect of the glen is one of animation and colour. The river runs through crevices and over rocks to the falls which cascade into limpid pools. I expected to hear a fairy story about this place and was surprised when I did not.

It was said, however, that fairies inhabit another dell in the vicinity called Glen Drink.

There are a whole series of charming glens between Laxey and Ramsey. Ballaglass, which we explored two or three days ago, is a happy hunting ground of photographers. I am told it frequently features in prize-winning pictures in the Tourist Board's annual photographic competition.

At Cornaa we saw a cottage which was the birthplace

of William Kennish, who devised a scheme to join the Atlantic and Pacific Oceans which was said to have been largely incorporated in the Panama Canal. He made the surveys forty years before the Panama Canal was built. Kennish is the most notable of the few inventors the Isle of Man has produced. He joined the Navy in 1825 when he was 22 because he had been jilted, and while in the Service made a number of inventions which were used by the Admiralty, for one of which he received the Gold Medal of the Society of Arts and Commerce. When steam began to be used as a means of motive power for ships he devised several marine engines and a screw propeller. He was also a poet, some of his work being published in a book entitled *Mona's Isle*.

Then we came to Corony Hill and the big 'Rest and Be Thankful' house at the top of the hill leading into Ramsey.

At the brick Town Hall, built in 1888, we were met by the astonishingly young and gay Mayor and Chairman, Mr. Garside, the local Member of the House of Keys, Mr. Kelly, and the Director of Publicity, Mr. Reubens, a very cheerful soul who has made the Atlantic crossing seventy-eight times and is going out again next month. These Manxmen are certainly globe-trotters.

While he plied us most generously with whisky and sherry Mr. Garside showed us photographs of Royalty at various times being welcomed at Ramsey. There were King George V and Queen Mary, and Queen Elizabeth, the Queen Mother. Ramsey has certainly earned her title of Royal Ramsey. Time and again, Royalties have put in to Ramsey because of their failure, owing to storms, to land at Douglas. It is a strange tradition that the Island is invariably enveloped in mist and storm when Royalty approaches. Doubtless in past ages Royalty was inseparably associated with the invader, and Mannanan-mac-y-lier, the protector, who threw his enshrouding spell over the Island to hide it from the hostile forces, evidently does not yet appreciate to the full that times have changed.

I was struck by the passionate local loyalty of our hosts. They have a town of which they have the right to be proud.

Mr. Reubens showed us a very fine new building estate of fifty-eight houses, another very attractive lot of houses specially built for elderly people, and then took us to the golf course, which lies within a few hundred yards of the centre of the town. This is an eighteen hole course over flat green land just below Sky Hill where the Island Championships are held. It is just the course for players who dislike climbing hills.

At the far end I saw the local Grammar School and the camp for the kilted Scots boys, who certainly add colour to the town.

He showed us the large slate quarries and the salt works, and told us that the brine was reputed to be the best for curing rheumatism in the world.

We drove by way of some small but extremely attractive modern houses and came to rest at the large yellow Hydro which stands at the north end of the town in splendid isolation, giving right on to a fine stretch of sands that are ideal for children. I found the dining-room packed out with youngsters. Ramsey is specially good for children, as the bathing is safe and they can go yachting on the model lake, which is nowhere more than four feet deep.

After luncheon we were shown the house where Anthony Quayle's family lived and the home of two other Island worthies, the Thellussons and the Bryants.

On the sea front we stopped to inspect the Catholic church dedicated to Our Lady of the Sea and St. Maughold, a very handsome building designed by Sir Giles Scott when he was very young. It contains some extremely fine, modern, stained glass windows depicting ships. Each of the stations of the Cross commemorates some local resident and there are fine paintings of the Last Supper and Our Lord's Baptism in a side chapel. The general colour scheme is bright blue and this extends to the Confessional Boxes and the gallery which is ornately decorated.

This is the finest church that I have so far seen in the Island. I had not realised before the strength of the Catholics here.

We passed the attractive yellow stone Court House and then crossed the Sulby River, which Mr. Reubens told us was prolific in big salmon.

We drove by two very happy-looking children's homes which have been acquired at a peppercorn rental, and then went down to the open-air swimming pool, which was the first ever to be built in the British Isles. It is almost as broad as it is long. In the same building is a large dance hall and restaurant. Here I saw a photograph of the bathing beauty to whom we gave first prize last week. Her name is Shirley Quayle.

As we drove out of the town we passed a colony of pleasant little houses, 'Earl's Court', Mr. Reubens called it, where retired English business men live frugally planting potatoes in their front gardens.

The outstanding feature of the town is its spaciousness. They have wisely built a miniature golf course along the northern end of the promenade and I saw a large number of tennis courts where the charges were only 1s. 6d. an hour.

The lake for model yachts occupies, I should say, quite a few acres, and everywhere I got the impression that it would be the easiest thing in the world to get away from the crowds if there were any.

In point of fact Ramsey is very quiet. I saw any number of sign-posted walks leading through the woods up to the hills. It is an ideal walking country with magnificent views everywhere over the Point of Ayre to Mull and to the Cumberland coast.

We spent a very pleasant afternoon driving through Ayre, which is a flattish nose of extraordinarily rich farm land. Mr. Reubens knew the name of every farm and told us stories about almost every one.

I saw flocks of very healthy-looking sheep, some right out on the headland, a good many cattle and field after field of ripening oats, not many of which had succumbed to the wild wind.

In the centre of Ayre we came to Bride Village, which stands on a hill and contains yet another of these solid-looking housing estates, for farm workers this time.

Many of the farms have long Dutch barns.

"You can always judge a farm," said Mr. Reubens, "by the size of its barns."

Mr. Reubens is a great sportsman and usually takes his pointer with him. He fishes all the glen waters and shoots woodcock at Ayre and wild duck in the Curragh.

Beyond Bride, which has an old church and a new reading room, we came to a long stretch of heather-covered, flat, low moor and then arrived at the tall lighthouse by the side of which is the place where they take in the brine. A larger industry is provided by the vast beach of shingle left by a rapidly-receding sea. This is sold to Port Sunlight, among other places, to be crushed into cement.

At the end of the Point I saw a gannet and three terns flying above a wicked-looking race of troubled waters known as the Strews.

After turning again inland we came first to the R.A.F. Station at Andreas, and then the bigger airport at Jurby, which occupy what was formerly the finest farm land in the Island. This area was known as the land of Canaan (flowing with milk, if not honey).

Andreas has an ancient village club and they still preserve the old custom of having a Procession on Ascension Day. We passed the only hotel in the extreme north of the Island.

I was surprised by the number of ponds we passed on this flat peninsula.

At one farm, Ballaratcliffe, there once lived a singularly independent farmer who insisted on wearing his hat in church, smoking during the service and stumping out during the sermon. Another farm was famous for two brothers who were said to have the best bass voices in the Island.

When the mist is too bad for aeroplanes to come down at Ronaldsway, passengers are landed at Jurby, which is still an active R.A.F. station for the training of cadets.

It is here that Mr. Reubens comes for mushrooms, which are to be found in profusion all over the Island, but in the greatest quantity here.

I noticed there were several thatched cottages in this area. I was told that the art of thatching is still carried on quite extensively here. Instead of straw, a type of grass brought from the Jurby shore is used, and is considered to last longer. One of these cottages was occupied by the last of the old Manx cottage weavers.

In one of the cottage gardens I saw myrrh growing. Most of the old cottagers think it lucky to have myrrh which they say bursts into bloom during the hours of darkness on Old Christmas Eve. It is lucky, of course, because of the association with the Magi. When the calendar was reformed two hundred years ago with the loss of eleven days, some of the old Manx communities refused to accept the new Christmas and right up to the beginning of this century observed Christmas on January 5th. Cregneish, near Port St. Mary, was one of the strongholds of the old Christmas. It used to be a practice to stay out until midnight to watch the myrrh flower. Apparently, a small white flower appears which dies before morning. The flowering type of myrrh has a strong smell.

One cottage which was pointed out to me had mud walls.

It was built in the sixteenth century and is the only one of its kind in the Island. Unfortunately, it is now in a state of decay.

We saw Jurby Church which is in a rather isolated position. Recently, a silver chalice which had been in the church since the early sixteenth century was sold to the Manx Museum by the churchwardens for £1000. It is one of the oldest pre-Reformation chalices in the British Isles and the oldest piece of silver in the Island.

We crossed two fields and scaled hedges which were riddled with rabbit holes to the point of collapse, to look at the roofless church dedicated to the patron saint of music, St. Cecilia. There were some beautiful carvings on the walls. The Manx name for it is St. Kickle, and a fair was held there on St. Cecilia's Day, November 9th.

There are more rabbits in this part than anywhere else in the Island. The ground is sandy, and the rabbits seem to do a lot of damage.

This is also the best type of soil for potatoes, and I was not surprised to hear that the best potatoes in the Island are grown in the north.

We also stopped at Ballachurry, a beautiful old estate with one of the finest avenues of trees along the drive that I have seen. The owner is a member of the Upper House of the Manx Parliament. About a quarter of a mile behind the house I saw the Ballachurry fort. The huge earth walls form a rectangle about 50 yards by 40 yards, with curiously shaped bastions on each corner. It was built about 1640 by James, the Seventh Earl of Derby. The purpose of it seems to be obscure.

We saw some beautiful chestnut trees in this part. The north of the Island is much more thickly wooded than the south. Trees probably grow better here, because of the protection from the prevailing wind given by the range of hills.

Injebreck
Valley

Ballaglass Glen

Another house of interest which was pointed out was Ellanbane, which was surrounded by a moat. It was the estate of Captain Myles Standish who sailed to America in the *Mayflower* with the Pilgrim Fathers. It is amazing how these Manxmen pop up everywhere.

"Was Standish a Manxman?" I asked. Well the Manx people believe he was. The evidence is that in his will he left his estate in the Isle of Man to his son, Alexander. The only Standishes in the Island then were at Ellanbane, and they were a Manx family whose records go back to 1504, when they were mentioned in the Manorial Roll of the Island, which is still preserved.

It has also been established that Captain Standish of the *Mayflower* married a Manx woman from Lezayre and took her to America. When she died he married her sister, which was, I thought, illegal in those days.

Another of the country estates in the district which I saw was Milntown, Lezayre, ancestral home of the Christian family. I have mentioned already two famous scions of the family, William Christian—Illiam Dhone—who surrendered the Island to the Roundheads, and Fletcher Christian, leader of the *Bounty* mutineers. They were a family of Scandinavian origin and one of them was a Deemster as far back as 1408. There were two more Deemsters in the line. One of them acquired Milntown, and the other was the first to put the Manx laws in writing. Ewan Christian, who succeeded to the Milntown property in 1593, was a Deemster when only 26 years old—the youngest ever—and held the office for 51 years—the longest ever. He was also the Deputy Governor of Peel Castle. Milntown is a fine old house standing back from the main Ramsey road at the top of a tree-lined drive.

We drove on to Sulby and once again climbed up the Glen. There are grouse moors on the top where Mr. Reubens told us a day's bag may well reach 60 birds.

There are plenty of rabbits, but no hares. Red squirrels too have been reported.

The mountain expanses and mountain roads of the Isle of Man remind me of North Wales. On a smaller scale they are very similar. The mountain range runs right through the centre like a backbone with dozens of ravines and small valleys breaking away from it. There are turbulent mountain streams which look like silver ribbons from the altitude of the higher mountain roads.

The roads form a network over the mountains in all directions. While our intrepid drivers took us over some very rough tracks we found, in the main, that the mountain roads and approaches through the valleys and glens were excellent. They make the most isolated parts of the Island easily accessible.

I discovered another characteristic that the Island—or rather its people—have in common with Wales. They are singers and actors. The Island is rich in choral societies and dramatic societies. They have a local musical festival in May for which everyone who can walk or ride turns out. They also go to the mainland to compete in the music festivals, and a drama festival is also held once a year, to which all comers are invited to compete and teams come from England and Ireland.

We stopped again at the Bungalow Restaurant on the T.T. course to drink a nip of whisky, saw the peat cuttings where Mr. Reubens told us diggers staked their claims, and sometimes left their turf overnight, to find it gone in the morning.

After dinner, we explored the various pierheads and joined a large crowd to see the Dublin passengers disembark. They have, of course, to go through the Customs.

The Victoria Pier is fitted with Radar. The screen is in a building at the end of the pier, and ships are guided into their berths in foggy weather by wireless telephone. The radar installation was fitted four or five years ago and brought Douglas right up to date. I was impressed with the efficient way that the crowds of passenger arrivals are handled at the piers.

The head offices of the Steam Packet Company are housed in what was once the leading hotel in the town. Alongside it is an old building which was once the Courthouse. It was called 'The Nineholes'.

I enquired for the Fort which gave the name of Fort Street to one of the streets down to the piers. I was told it was at the base of the Victoria Pier but had been demolished. It was there up to the beginning of the eighteenth century and was manned by the parishioners of Braddan (which then included Douglas) on a sort of conscription system. It seems that practically all Manxmen were liable for military service. A favoured few who were exempt included 'The Twenty Four'—the members of the House of Keys.

The fort on the Victoria Pier was said to be one of the oldest in the British Isles. An old historian said that Caractactus, the brother of Boadicea, concealed his young nephew from the Romans in this fort. There was said to be an underground compartment in it known as 'The Great Man's Chamber'. As far as I could see it is likely that the crowds of holiday-makers pass over it on the way from the steamers.

WEDNESDAY   *Peel—Sheep Dog Trials,*
                    Quarter Bridge—The T.T. Course

Today I was able, for the first time, to sit at the open window in the sun, to do my early morning work. I wake much later than I do at home, about 5.30 or even six instead of 3.30 or four. There is no question whatever about the invigorating power of this air. It also induces good sleep at night.   Jill sleeps happily on until about eight, which is rare for her, and I haven't slept till six for over a year. Today the glass has risen and for the first time the wind has dropped.   How stealthily ships creep in and out of the bay.   I looked up this morning to see a destroyer lying at anchor about halfway across the bay.   She belongs to the new 'Daring' class.   Her name is *Duchess*.   She is in for a courtesy visit for a week.

By strong contrast we saw also a timber ship of blueygreen and yellow masts, loaded to the brim, *Sine Boye*, from Mastral which, from her red and white flag, I took to be Swedish.   Somebody said Norway, but I'm pretty sure that Norway flies a red and black or red and blue ensign.

We caught the 9.50 bus for Peel, for which there was a large queue, as it was a bright and sunny day.

These buses start off on the dot to a whistle, but they travel slowly and they are rightly very careful about stopping at 'Halt' signs, of which there are far more in a small area than I have ever seen anywhere else.

I was more than ever struck by the extreme neatness and cleanliness everywhere.   It is the more noticeable because of the newly put on white-wash and yellow-wash.   In many of the tall Victorian lodging houses in the Peel Road leading out of the town I saw 'Vacancies' notices in the window.   So far, the season has been relatively quiet.

At the Tynwald I noticed what I had failed to see before. In addition to the tall pole that surmounts the mound containing the soil of all seventeen parishes, there is a tall war memorial between the mound and the church, which is one of the few churches in the Island with a high spire.

There wasn't much traffic on the road, but we passed one runner.   I have never been able to understand the pleasure of running on a tarmac road, as it jars all the leg muscles, and you can't admire the scenery because of the highbanked hedges.

When we came to the city of Peel it took a little time to find the Town Hall.   One woman in a shop said, "Are you being sarcastic ?   We call it the Food Office."

Indeed, it is an inconspicuous building in a narrow ancient street.   I was delighted to find a warm coal fire.

"St. Swithin's Day," explained the Town Clerk, Mr. Kelly, "a form of protection."

He introduced me to a tall, elderly, retired bank manager, Mr. Thomas Dodd, a man of great learning and charm, who talks Manx and quoted many Manx proverbs, the most notable being, "When the poor help the poor, God laughs in approval."

We were taken first across the road to Curtis's herring factory, where we watched a woman take herrings out of a case and place them one by one upon a rotating machine which slit them, gutted them and washed them.

We then saw the brine bath in which they were immersed for an hour, and then watched some half a dozen workers spreading them flat on to hooks on sticks in strings of a dozen and then they were taken to be smoked over a slow fire of oak chippings for a period that seemed to vary between eighteen and twenty-four hours.

In another part of the factory a man was gutting dog-fish.

Mr. Dodd told me that there were three hundred Peel fishing boats when he was a boy, but that today the native fishing had declined and that they no longer built drifters or even made nets.   The great days of the Peel fishing fleet are described by Hall Caine in *The Deemster*.   Now, all but three of the many boats in the harbour came by way of the Caledonian Canal from Leith, Kirkcaldy, and other Scottish ports.   They arrive in June and leave again in September.

Most of their haul is caught just outside Peel, or off the Calf of Man.   They go out about eight o'clock at night, when the fish begin to leap up out of the water, and come in at dawn. The fish go to the bottom in daytime.

We went down to the harbour to see the herrings being drawn up in quarter cran baskets which were so generously laden that herrings glided off into the water. Others fell or were thrown on to the quay where hundreds of gulls fought for them, and I saw gulls swallow these herrings whole. As a gull weighs only about ten to twelve ounces, it must swallow many times its own weight at every meal.

The Scots drifters are handsome boats and the fishermen a grand, sober-looking lot of men. There is a crew of about six in each ship. With them I noticed a Lowestoft steam trawler which had put into the harbour.

Mr. Kelly told me that the fishermen like to spend their leisure hours on board and only go ashore to attend dances and, of course, to go the rounds of the pubs.

I watched the fishermen mending their nets and idly smoking in groups, and then turned back along the quay to inspect the brand-new lifeboat *Helena Harris*, built at a cost of £31,000. She is a very handsome affair, forty feet long and fitted with fine engines and all the latest gadgets.

Outside the lifeboat house I saw the rather gaudily-painted figure-head of a Norwegian sailor, all that is left of the *St. George*, that was wrecked on the rocks just outside Fenella's Leap, below Peel Castle.

We spent a good deal of time going round the ruins of Peel Castle, the main buildings of which are of pink sandstone. It occupies the small St. Patrick's Isle which, originally separate, is now connected with the mainland by a stone causeway. This also serves to protect the entrance to the harbour and, as I mounted the stone step to look over the wall to the seaward side, it was quite a thrill to see on one side of this the tumultuous seas breaking against the rocks at the base of the castle, and on the other the calm harbour water.

In some ways the castle reminds me of Tintagel, though it doesn't stand so high above the water.

At its entrance is an interesting sundial.

The Cathedral is particularly striking with its three Early English, tall, narrow windows in the east end and a memorial to Bishop Rutter, with a Latin inscription which invites passers-by to stop and laugh at the thought of a Bishop reduced to a diet for worms. An unusually macabre epitaph.

The grave of Bishop Rutter, who died in 1662, was discovered by archaeologists in 1865 and one of them took the skull away. The story goes that, not long after, the possessor sickened and died. The skull subsequently got into the possession of a number of people and in every case misery and death followed. Finally, it became the property of the High Bailiff of Peel, who also became sick from a mysterious malady and was given up by the doctors. Then the High Bailiff's wife discovered the trail of death which had followed the skull, and had it buried again in Peel Castle. The High Bailiff then recovered.

Bishop Rutter was a friend of the great Earl of Derby. He was said to have written poetry for the amusement of his friend, and it was popular in the Island right up to the last century.

Two of the Norse Kings of Mann are reputed to have died in Peel Castle. The remains of one, Godred, were taken to Iona, and the other, Olave, was buried in Rushen Abbey.

Mr. Kelly showed us the place where the daylight ghost of a fisherman occasionally appears and then we went down to the crypt in which a Duchess of Gloucester was reputed to have been imprisoned. We then walked round the stout ramparts, which are made of grey stone and overlook the jagged rocks below.

We saw the Tilting Ground, now used for sports, the barracks, the summer residence of the Lords of Mann,

Earls of Derby, the place from which Fenella leapt (if we are to rely on *Peveril of the Peak*), a little roofless church, with Saxon herring-bone brick work, the circular Half Moon Battery, several ancient culverin, the machicolated Keep and a tall tower in the middle, the last refuge when the rest of the castle had been taken. There was a tablet commemorating the place where Edward VII and Queen Alexandra had signed their names in 1902.

We then returned along the causeway to the town and went around the white-washed walls of the old church, derelict since 1882, and after seeing the Catholic Church, climbed to the very handsome modern church, which is capable of seating a thousand people.

It originally was proposed to build a spire one hundred and eighty feet high, but it was found not to be strong enough and indeed, in the hurricane of 1903, the roof fell in and was completely destroyed.

After luncheon at the Palatine, we went down to the promenade to see the havoc caused by the great gale on the night when the *Princess Victoria* went down, early in 1953. Just here are some splendid tennis courts and bowling greens.

We then went by way of narrow medieval streets to the wonderful new Junior School, which cost £100,000. It is of one storey only, with large windows giving out on to the sea on one side, and on to the mountains on the other. The Headmaster showed us the Big Hall in which children were dancing, and then took us through the Dining Hall to the ultra-modern kitchens.

Peel is a quite unsophisticated, unpretentious resort with fine sands. Grand walks over the hills have been acquired by the National Trust or the local authorities in order to provide free cliff walks as far as Glen Maye.

The old part of the town consists of narrow, winding streets, with quaint little houses, many of them very old, which are full of cellars and riddled with tunnels which were used by smugglers. The Isle of Man, it seems, was the centre of a thriving business in illicit liquor for over one hundred years.

It was started by adventurers from Liverpool around 1670, who realised the possibilities of the Island as a distributing centre and cashed in on it. Before long, the trade increased until whole cargoes were brought to the Island and 'run' to England, Ireland and Scotland. Respectable local merchants took up the business and sent their ships to France and Spain for wines and spirits which were legitimately imported into the Island and the small Manx duty paid on them. Then they were sold to the smugglers. The merchants held that their trade was legitimate and even appointed a deputation to go to London and put their point of view to the chagrined Imperial Government.

The trade was eventually brought to an end by the sale of the customs rights on the Island by the Duke of Atholl to the British Crown for £70,000. British customs officers were sent to the Island and empowered to board all ships, including Manx vessels, lying off the harbours and to seize all forms of contraband. It was a black day for the hundreds engaged in the business, especially the merchants, who had grown prosperous on it.

I saw an example of cobblestone mosaic in front of an old cottage. It is a method of paving the yards by making a design with stones brought from the beach. Someone had put a lot of work into it. Grey and white stones were woven into an intricate design.

Further up this street, which was the old road into Peel, I saw the cottage of Philip Christian, who founded the Clothworkers School of Peel. He died in 1652 and left bequests for the education of the youth of Peel.

There is a striking contrast between the very new and the very old in this ancient and honourable city.

We caught the two o'clock bus in order to be in time to attend the Sheep Dog Trials in the immense meadow at Quarter Bridge, known as Port-e-chee.

There was a huge concourse of spectators round three sides of the field, with a well-filled grandstand on the southern side, where a place was found for us in the front row, among the sheep dogs and competitors, several of whom were speaking Welsh, by Mr. Howie, the Agricultural Organiser for the Isle of Man Board of Agriculture and Fisheries.

Some six or ten sheep were let loose eight hundred yards away, where a white flag was raised. First we watched the 'Singles', in which one black and white sheep dog was released to dash first for its half mile sprint, to round up the flock and bring the sheep through a distant gate and then, closer to us, to negotiate gates on either side of the field; then to pass through two narrow passages in the shape of a Maltese Cross; then to separate; and finally to be penned.

The sheep were, for the most part, stubborn, petulant and refractory, stamping their feet with annoyance and standing broadside on or with their backs to the passages and the pen. But the farmers, with infinite patience, coaxed and cajoled them, waving their shepherd's crooks and giving orders to their wily and watchful dogs by means of high-pitched whistles and phrases like 'ahint there' and 'lie down', and others which to me meant nothing.

We saw competitions between Manx farmers and also international affairs, in which England, Scotland and Wales each had two representatives.

The most successful competitors were those who kept the sheep quiet and more or less unconscious of what they were doing.

One of the most interesting features was the intelligent way in which the dogs who were resting at my feet kept an eye on all that was going on, nodding approval or dis-approval at the manoeuvres of the working dogs.

The singles championship was won by a Derbyshire farmer, T. E. Elliot, and the local championship by Norman Crowe.

After Sir Mark Collett had presented the cups, we watched A. E. Priestley drive half a dozen ducks between a series of posts in a sort of slalom race which evoked considerable laughter, as ducks invariably look ridiculous as they strive in vain to maintain a sense of dignity when being coerced by dogs to go in any given direction.

The dogs, with one exception, were models of obedience, instantly obeying their master's voices.

On leaving the meadow we walked to Kirk Braddan to inspect the old church, which contains a dozen very interesting old crosses, many of them Scandinavian, inscribed with crude figures and runes. These range from the sixth to the twelfth centuries and include Odd's Cross, Thorstein's Cross, Thorleif Hunkki's Cross and Roskitil Cross. On Odd's Cross is the inscription 'Odd raised this Cross to his father Frakki but Thorbjorn . . .' There it stops. The rest is indecipherable.

This church has horse-box pews, and a fine old grey stone tower with open belfry. The pews rise at the west end below a gallery, and the walls and ceiling are white-washed. The churchyard lies among tall trees and contains a large number of interesting tombstones, one of which has a sculptured hand holding a heart.

The entrance is on Braddan Bridge, one of the most spectacular corners of the T.T. course. Against the wall of the church I saw the gravestone of a former Vicar which, according to the dates on it, was erected fourteen years before his death. The Rev. Robert Brown, father of the Manx poet, T. E. Brown, is also buried there. The finest Runic cross in the Island is in this church.

Kirby Park, near the church, is a picturesque estate. The house was built by Sir Mark Wilks, who was Governor of St. Helena for the East India Company part of the time that Napoleon Bonaparte was exiled there. He received Napoleon on his arrival and Napoleon is said to have got on well with him. He later became Speaker of the House of Keys. He had a beautiful daughter named Laura, with whom one of Napoleon's generals, Baron Gourgaud, who went into exile with him, fell violently in love.

At the entrance to the churchyard there is a wide stone or slate stile, very much like the stiles I associate with Cornwall. It is an eerie place practically hidden among trees.

We walked home along the high road and when we got back to Douglas we inspected the fishermen's church, St. Matthew's, which is an ornate High Church, with many pictures and a smell of incense.

At dinner, the quite silent couple sitting behind me were drinking their usual bottle of Dry Monopole, and Mr. Cahn had as guests Captain Fry-Goldie-Taubman and Mrs. Cunliffe-Owen.

As it was such a clear night, Mr. and Mrs. Drinkwater drove us, after dinner, to see their new home at Union Mills, which has a lovely series of French windows, and stands high looking out south over meadow land to the hills above the sea. It is a quiet, very attractive two-storeyed converted farm.

We then drove right round the T.T. course, which gave me some slight idea of the endurance, quite apart from the courage, required by the competitors.

This course is $37\frac{3}{4}$ miles round. It goes from Douglas to Ramsey and back in a circular tour, going by Kirkmichael and Ballaugh on the west coast and returning over the slopes of Snaefell. It is covered seven times and the winners average speeds of over 90 miles an hour. In view of the many steep hills and hair-pin bends, this means, of course, that these daring motor-cyclists go very much more than that in many places.

As we motored round in Mr. Drinkwater's car at our more leisurely, but considerably safer, pace I was able, in my imagination, and thanks to the illustrated guide published by Messrs. Castrol, to follow the course at the more exciting speeds recommended by that well-known champion, Geoff Duke. Apparently the race starts at the good fast pace of 129 miles per hour down Bray Hill, then, after clipping the kerb (to use Duke's words) round the sharp corner at Quarter Bridge, it slows down to a steady 85 to 90 miles per hour at Union Mills, where we joined it. The tricky corners at Greeba Bridge and the Ballacraine Hotel are negotiated at between 45 and 60 miles per hour, and Laurel Bank at 60 to 80, and so on at similar speeds. Duke has no nonsense with the downhill bend at the 11th milestone, which he recommends without hesitation as being taken at 120 miles an hour, accelerating. This is merely warming up for the fastest section of the course at the 13th milestone, which he recommends covering at 130 miles per hour. Kirkmichael, however, demands caution and a mere 75 to 80, and he has a few warning words to say about the hump-backed bridge at Ballaugh, where the machines leave the ground altogether. He emphasises the importance of a 'two-point landing' here, not without reason, I should imagine, as the alternative to this must be a pretty grim one. Through Quarry Bend's a series of curves have to be taken at 100 miles per hour, then at Ginger Hill, while travelling at 70, it is apparently necessary to lift the head at an unnatural angle to avoid hitting the telegraph pole at the near corner.

It was the rather morbid fascination of this telegraph pole that distracted me from my detailed attention to the next stages of the course through Ramsey and, as we climbed up through Gooseneck, I soothed my blood-curdling thoughts by my interest in the glorious sunset, which showed up the whole of the Mull of Galloway silhouetted against the sky-line. As Jill remarked, it looked exactly like Ischia seen from Capri.

I have never seen such vivid light green colours on the sea. One could see, too, the massifs of the Merrick and the other mountains of Carrick, as well as the low-lying foreshore of Dumfries. In spite of the clear sky overhead, the tops of the Island mountains were wreathed in white wisps of cloud and a thin tablecloth of white just covered the top of South Barrule. At one stage we looked down on the whole wide bay of Ramsey.

After passing over the side of Snaefell, we looked down on the wide valley that leads to Douglas, whose front was, by this time, brilliantly lit up. We cautiously traversed the hairpin bend at Governor's Bridge (which even Duke recommends at 8 to 10 miles per hour) and so back to the Fort Anne Hotel.

THURSDAY   *A Wet Day*

I was woken by the fog-horn and again by a violent downpour of rain. After last night's unforgettably lovely sunset I thought we were in for a spell of fine weather. I suppose the fact that the Mull of Galloway stood out so clearly was a fatal sign. Bad weather seems always to succeed clear views.

It was too wet to do anything but work in the morning, but in the afternoon we went to a matinée (if wet only) at the Crescent, a magnificent ultra-modern cinema, the interior of which is constructed to look like a medieval fortress, with walls hung with very clever imitations of tapestry painted on either side. There was a portcullis, loopholes for cross-bows and all the gadgets one associates with castles, from heavy wooden beams to stout stone walls.

The film was *Moulin Rouge*, which gave a lurid picture of Paris in the 'nineties', purporting to illustrate the life of the drunken cripple, Toulouse-Lautrec. The best part was the reproduction of scores of Lautrec's paintings. The prices of seats were low, the highest being 2s. 6d., and the house was packed.

At 7.15, Mr. and Mrs. Bond called for us and drove us to the Golf Links Hotel, Castletown, the castellated building which stands at the edge of the well-known golf links at the end of the peninsula, which contains a bird sanctuary and the Langness Lighthouse. The hotel is smart, and was full of enthusiastic golfers in club ties, who go round as many as three times a day and look as bronzed and hearty as golfers usually do. They surprised me by demanding the blinds to be drawn at dinner to keep out the sun and, incidentally, the very lovely views over the rocky coves, airport and the mountain of South Barrule. The fare was excellent and I was specially pleased with the novel notion of printing the waitress's Christian name on a ticket on the table.

After dinner we drove by a gated, rough track past many deserted buildings over the bird sanctuary, where I heard ringed plover and oyster catchers piping over the dunes and down by the rocky shore.

This is a place to which tourists rarely penetrate, so the golfers have their Paradise to themselves and rarely leave the links until it is time to settle down to bridge after dinner. A very restful place, but I saw no children, all of whom seem to concentrate on Port Erin. I doubt if children would be popular in these surroundings.

Indeed, the sea bathing here is not good owing to the number of rocks, but the hotel has a private swimming pool. The boating is also not too good as it is difficult to land at low tide.

Nearer to King William's College, which faces right on

to the beach at the mainland end of the peninsula, is another hotel that is run by the same company as the Fort Anne. Its name is the Derby Haven, and it stands close to the beach on which the first Derby was run.

As the first Derby was run on the Island you would expect horse-racing to be among the most popular of Manx sports.

In fact, gambling on both horse-racing and dog-racing is now illegal, but the Islanders are certainly proud to remember that as long ago as 1630 the Earl of Derby instituted a race run over a piece of land on Langness still known as the Racecourse, which was undoubtedly the forerunner of the Epsom Derby. Started by the seventh Earl, it was continued after the Restoration by the eighth Earl, and you can still see the rules for the race drawn up in 1669 that are now housed in the Rolls Office. In the 1687 race, among the five entries were the Deemster (one of the famous Christian family) and the Governor, Robert Heywood. The Governor won.

Lord Derby's idea was obviously to popularise the Manx ponies, which were both strong and speedy. Indeed, in the eighteenth century many Manxmen became celebrated riders and there was a good deal of competition between parishes.

According to Canon Stenning, all wedding days were the occasion of a race. The young men took their horses to the church and tied them to the churchyard railings. When the service was over, they raced to the home of the bride and the first man to reach her door was allowed to break the wedding cake over her head as she came into the house.

As, on our way home, we passed the white Fairies Bridge, everyone in the car said "Goodnight, Little People", which I hope will modify any ill consequence of my having seen the new moon through the window of the car.

When we got back to the hotel we found that the

Castle Rushen, Castletown

Peel Castle

Duchess was giving a very generous, even dazzling, display of fireworks.

A man standing behind me on the terrace said, "There goes all my income tax."

Indeed, they seemed to have so many flares and rockets to spare that I could only believe that they must have been left over from the Naval Coronation Review.

FRIDAY   *Snaefell—The Aquarium, Port Erin*

I was woken up by a couple of claps of thunder in the night, but it came to nothing. It turned out to be a wild, windy and wet day, so we spent it in running round the island by train, tram and bus. I watched the week-end exodus in the steamers at breakfast-time.

Queues about a quarter of a mile long filed slowly along the pier-heads to the five steamers and then vanished into the depths of the ships.

We caught the 10.15 from the station, which has an unexpectedly well-equipped bar and handsome waiting-rooms.

Only the first-class compartments are upholstered all the way up. The train went much faster than I expected and only stopped for a few seconds at each station.

First we passed through a land of wide meadows full of cattle and sheep, and at St. John's the front part of the train went on to Peel, while we turned northward up the west coast towards Ramsey. We were soon running high along the cliff edge with a fine view over the sea towards Ireland. We saw a large camp in a protected place in Glen Wyllin, which stands just below Kirkmichael and here most of the passengers got out. I noticed that the oats in this part of the Island have been badly blown about.

At Sulby Glen there were a number of glass-houses containing carnations.

8

We reached Ramsey at 11.40, and after looking at some rather good shops, caught the twelve o'clock electric tram for Laxey. This climbed steeply up past Mrs. Cunliffe-Owen's fine new house. Once again I noticed that the superb sands at Ramsey were completely deserted at mid-day.

We stopped at a number of halts, among them Deemskerry for Port Moar, a lovely cove, and got an increasingly good view of the east coast as we passed the great variety of deep glens, Ballaglass, Mona and Dhoon, before coming to the cliff edge overlooking Laxey. This cliff scenery is remarkably wild and picturesque, with heather growing out of the steep slate screes.

We reached Laxey at 12.45 and went straight to the Bridge Hotel, where a number of visitors were singing as they drank. Jill had one boiled egg and I had two. I drank a whiskey and Jill drank cider. They also brought a pot of tea which we hadn't ordered. The charge with bread and butter was 9s. 1d.

At 1.30 we caught an electric tram for the summit of Snaefell. This journey took about three quarters of an hour and we looked out on the narrow steep gorge down which runs the Laxey River, and above it a pleasant green track leading to the deserted lead mines.

The big wheel of Laxey was working. It is called The Lady Isabella and is seventy-two feet in diameter. It takes half a minute to make a complete revolution and I was told that when it was working it raised two hundred and fifty gallons of water a minute from the mines at a depth of three hundred fathoms. About six hundred men were employed in the Laxey mines.

Laxey, of course, has its own glen, with specially attractive gardens and a small boating pool. There is also an open-air arena in which they have dancing and boxing.

We stopped for tickets to be collected at the Bungalow

Hotel on the T.T. course and then began a circuit of the mountain. At the top we saw a small hotel and had to walk about two hundred yards to the summit (2,034 feet), where stands a radar station and an Ordnance Survey stone.

The views on all sides of the mountain were superb, but storm clouds obliterated the south and before we regained the shelter of the tram the rain reached us. We were only on the top about ten minutes and before we regained the Bungalow the top of the mountain was shrouded in mist and the rain poured down.

This did not prevent other visitors from going up, for all the trams we passed on our way down were full.

When we got down to Laxey we ran for a bus and on reaching the bus station at Douglas went straight on by another bus to Port Erin, at 3.40, in order to see the Aquarium, where there is also a fish hatchery and biological station founded in 1902.

We didn't get much time there as they shut at five o'clock, and we arrived at 4.45.

It is small but extraordinarily interesting. I saw a tank containing two enormous conger-eels, one standing on its head, the other with its head hidden in a rock. Round them played several cuckoo wrasse rather affectionately, certainly quite fearlessly. I was surprised to see how slow is the growth of plaice and lobsters. I saw them in various stages from one day old upwards, and they seem to remain minute specks for ages. I learnt that nearly 200,000,000 plaice have been hatched here in the last fifty years. Their rate of mortality in the sea is quite stupendous and in view of their size I am not surprised.

We saw fish labelled 'walking', 'swimming', 'attached' and 'burrowing'. There were large lobsters immured with every variety of other fish, which seemed to take no notice of each other. These were spotted dogfish, gurnards, octopi, skate, very graceful lemon soles and dabs dancing a sort of ballet, and many coloured anemones as well as smaller fry, prawns, and so on. In addition to the hatcheries, there were also models of drifters showing the way the nets worked, and stuffed gannets and black throated divers.

When we got back to the harbour we saw four drifters from Dunure, *Stormdrift* and *Summer Rose* were the names of two of them, just setting out. A large liner passed just outside the harbour and we saw, as usual, the Mountains of Mourne.

In spite of passing storms, the flat sea-wall was well patronised and there were scores of bathers and hundreds of families lying out in deck chairs. Once again I was impressed by the quiet serenity of the holiday makers at Port Erin who seem much more relaxed than the restless wanderers along the front at Douglas.

We caught the last train out of Port Erin, which left at 5.35. This took us first to Port St. Mary and then inland along a marshy area by way of Castletown to Port Soderick, where we got a good view of the coast walk where the trams used to run.

The journey by train took about an hour and I was fascinated by the toy engines, *Fenella* and *Kissack*, which go at unexpectedly high speed and indulge in as much whistling as if they were being driven by small boys.

SATURDAY   *A Walk to Port Soderick*

The glass rose in the night and the day was fine with a fresh wind and plenty of sun. We had to spend the greater part of the morning indoors working, but in the early hours I had heard the steamers arrive from Glasgow (it is the Glasgow Fair week) and at breakfast I saw the queues forming up in processions at least a quarter of a mile long waiting to embark.

When we went out at noon we saw the promenade

crowded with Scots, most of them lying prone in the sun asleep after their night voyage, many of them in deck chairs on the beach, some playing ball on the sands, and a few bathing.

After luncheon we took a further walk along the sea coast track past Douglas Head, which had formerly been the tramway to Port Soderick. The water below was clear and blue and the rocks were full of seagulls who were making a tremendous noise. We met about a dozen people in the five miles, which was very pleasant walking.

Twice we had to make a detour because of dangerous bridges closed off by barbed wire. To negotiate the first gully we had to descend steps on one side and then climb up the other. The second was more formidable as the bridge crossed a steep cliff. This necessitated climbing a steep track over the heather-covered moor above the cliffs. Below we saw two hardy or foolhardy men taking the wide way that led to possible destruction. We preferred the straight and safer way over the hill.

One deep ravine had the curious name of the Horse Leap. The story is that a man on horseback and some dogs were chasing a hare which ran over the edge of the ravine and the dogs were unable to halt their progress and went after it. The horseman, however, whipped his steed and cleared the gully to safety. It is fully fifteen yards wide and a prodigious leap for any horse.

Near the Horse Leap are two rocks of weird formation, again with a curious name, The Nun's Chairs. They stand out to sea at high tide but can be reached from the rocks when the tide is low. They are said to have been used as a barbarous form of punishment for erring nuns who were made to sit on them while the tide flowed and ebbed twice.

There were a few couples lying on the steep banks of bracken and heather, but the exquisite coves below were untenanted.   They seemed to be inaccessible until we came to Keristal, where we found a modern café, where we had an early tea.   To my surprise everyone was having tea indoors, presumably because it was too hot to sit in the sun.   Just below Keristal I saw two very attractive coves and on the beach there were three of four people playing, though how they got down remained a mystery.   I saw no path.

While we were standing there, three motor-boats came round the coast from Douglas with aspiring conger-eel fishers.

I don't know whether the conger-eels at Port Soderick are specially numerous or specially large, but they get all the publicity so far as the advertised trips in search of them are concerned.

I understand that there is an Annual Angling Festival in the Island in September which lasts for a week and a number of trophies and shields are awarded for the heaviest conger, flounder, ling, mackerel, pollack and wrasse, the heaviest catch in rock events and pier competitions, as well as for the heaviest fish caught at Langness, Scarlett or Niarbyl.   There is also a cup for juniors under 15.

In the last few years, two British Isles records were set up with fish caught in these waters.   One was a brill of 16 lb. caught near Langness and the other a mackerel of over 4 lb. caught at Peel Pier.

The rules for these competitions seem to be simple enough.   The tackle in use has to be one Rod, Reel and Running Line, with a maximum of three hooks or one triangle.   No fish can be landed by hand-lining, but netting and gaffing are permitted.

When we came to the end of the track we descended by a steep narrow path to the cove which struck me as un-deservedly neglected.   There was an artificial concrete way called the Marine Parade, which led by stone steps to a

Wishing Well, Smuggler's Caves and two or three delightful bathing beaches, where at high tide you could dive into deep clear blue water.

We watched the motor launches set out from the slipway on their return voyage, and then walked up the wide road to the station, which stands delightfully among trees at the top of a densely wooded glen.

We only just resisted the temptation to take a train which was going to Port Erin.

Our train came in about five o'clock and soon we were back in Douglas, where we walked down the promenade and watched the hungry guests collecting at every boarding house doorway, waiting for the gong to sound for high tea, which they take at 5.30.

After dinner we walked to the end of the pier below the hotel to watch a group of fishermen who caught nothing. We could see several smallish fish swimming about in the clear water, but they were wary of the hook and line.

By the time we went to bed all the seven steamers had come into their haven of refuge for the week-end.

Pretty well everything shuts down on Sunday. There are few trains and the buses go infrequently. I particularly lament the closing of the bars.

SUNDAY   *Port St. Mary*

The glass rose very high and the day was sunny and bright until the afternoon.

We went to St. Matthew's for the sung Eucharist service at 11 a.m. It is called the fishermen's church, but there were no fishermen there. In fact, the congregation was very small, less than fifty, but the Service was carried out with elaborate ritual with acolytes, bells ringing, servers and much genuflection.

I was surprised to read in the special book provided

that the bell rang to bring back the inattentive to the solemnity of the service and there was a phrase "Do not be ashamed of your mother tongue", which struck me as inappropriate, for if there ever was a race of people who are proud and tenacious of their regional dialect, it is the Lancastrian.

I really prefer a quiet Communion without singing at eight o'clock, for at this High Mass no one celebrates except the Priest.

The sermon by Father Woods was simple, extempore and satisfying, and was on the subject of man's Free Will.

We found the beach and Promenade thronged with visitors who seemed to be wearing their Sunday best. Many of the men wore coloured shirts. Their suits were, for the most part, new. There were a few girls in white tennis shorts, more in jeans and trousers, most in print frocks. Very few were bathing. The majority relaxed in deck-chairs. A very large number were rowing round the bay.

At 12.45 there was a quick exodus, packing up of deck-chairs and a long procession to the boarding houses.

After luncheon we heard four rockets fired and very soon the lifeboat went out northwards across the bay. We heard afterwards that someone had been taken ill in a small yacht and needed a doctor, so the yacht came back with the lifeboat and the sick man was handed over to the doctor.

We joined an enormous queue at two o'clock for the 2.30 bus for Port St. Mary, which we had already found to be a very attractive 'poopy' sort of sandy bay with its two harbours. There were a large number of sailing boats lying up in the inner harbour and three or four drifters moored up alongside the long arm of the outer harbour. We watched fishermen aboard the *Manx Fairy* and *Maid of Erin* and a yacht called *Cordailys*. The cost of each drifter is approximately £8,000.

There were half a dozen fishermen angling off the end of the pier for pollack, wrasse and mackerel. They were not so successful as the anglers off Peel Pier.

At the southern end of the harbour we saw two old ladies reading and several couples lying on enormous flat slabs of rock rather like the Giant's Causeway in miniature, and we then walked round the point to the inlet of Perwick Bay. The coast here is wild and rocky and we watched several motor-boats coming back from the trip to the Calf of Man.

There are golf links on the rising ground leading towards Spanish Head and we saw one very handsome, stout house of stone, with wrought iron gates called Casa del Mar.

We then walked along a low esplanade below some ancient fishermen's cottages, which were built on a steep rocky bank.

The inner bay has an oyster-shaped sandy beach. There is perfect bathing below a stone wall with a promenade, the feature of which is a row of four-storeyed boarding houses and one large yellow hotel, the Balqueen Hydro.

We had tea in a pleasant, light, airy cafe called Cowley's. We watched a number of small children come in and were delighted by the courtesy and kindliness of the proprietor who took tremendous trouble in helping them to choose, even when their spending money was only one penny. This was a real throwback to the good days of the old village stores, when the shopkeeper had time to be genial and loved gossiping with his customers.

We inspected the solid modern church of St. Mary's, and were on our way to the terminus to catch the 5.45 bus when Mr. Cahn passed us in his car and gave us a lift home by the coast road.

Just outside Port St. Mary we drove beside the long wall that hid a large estate, and on the further side of Castletown he showed us the oldest farm in the Island, which has barns that date back to the eighth century.

As soon as we got home the clouds came up, the rain fell and it became suddenly cold, so we stayed indoors.

A very gay party of French men and women arrived at the hotel in time for dinner. They drank a lot of wine and were very hilarious. I was told that they were a party of eighteen, a French choir who were due to sing at the Villa Marina.

MONDAY   *King William's College—*
                                            Rushen Abbey

A most remarkable day of combined high gale, high seas, drenching rain and almost complete invisibility. I always thought before that mists and gales were incompatible, but on this day the Island was blanketed during the entire day, so the fog-horns sounded incessantly and the aeroplanes due to leave and land at Ronaldsway were diverted to Jurby.

But in spite of this and the uncomfortable fact that I was seized with a violent grippe, we covered a great deal of ground.

We were called for by Mr. Faragher, an enthusiastic member of the staff of the Tourist Board. Formerly a motor salesman, he now sells the Isle of Man. He spends very little of his time in the Isle of Man—the greater part of the year he is working in England and Scotland, trying to induce the people to come to the Isle of Man for their summer holidays.

His activities are numerous and range from giving film shows in factories to running Isle of Man dances in the large dance halls in the various cities of the north. There would appear to be never a dull moment in Mr. Faragher's life.

I am only sorry that he and I did not team up earlier in

my career as a travel writer. We could have had quite a time. As it is, I fear that I am something of a late-comer to the Beauty Queen game and, as I have already confessed, my Victorian upbringing would be a permanent handicap.

We drove first through the blinding rain to the Castletown Nautical Museum, erected above the schooner *Peggy*, which was built and sailed by Captain Walter Quayle in 1769, a very staunch boat some forty feet long, which is kept in perfect condition, walled-in just above the busy harbour.

The curator showed us a room shaped exactly like a poop deck. This contained Quayle's Bank ledger. This belonged to George Quayle, whom I have already mentioned as keeping a private bank. He issued his own 'card' money, which he was willing enough to give out but reluctant to take back. The walls were hung with bills of lading, where I saw that a boy earned 6d. a day and that rum cost 4s. 6d. a gallon. One of his bills amounted to £101, so he obviously had a prosperous business. Many of the names of his employees were Lancastrian, brought over doubtless by the Stanleys, who evidently relied on the henchmen from the Derby estate for their labour.

There were some very interesting maps dating back to Saxon days, a copy of the first book to be printed in Manx, and a Ramsey Prayer Book dated 1769. There was a plan of a diamond-shaped raft designed by Napoleon to contain thirty thousand men for the invasion of England, which aroused the mirthful contempt of the curator, as he said that it would only drift in any direction the sea liked to take it, and was impossible to steer in any given direction. He also showed us a permit for Quayle to enter certain harbours. There were several small culverin lying about upstairs and we saw the sailmaker's loft.

We then drove on to King William's College, where the

Headmaster (Mr. Wilson), his wife and son (just down from Pembroke College, Cambridge) showed us over the entire buildings.

Among the school's more famous pupils have been Sir William Bragg, Dean Farrar, T. E. Brown, 'Skipper' Lynam, who founded the Dragon School, Oxford, Sir George White, V.C., the defender of Ladysmith, and Thomas Fowler.

We were first taken over the chapel, an isolated building with paintings done on zinc to prevent the sea air from causing them to peel. There are many modern stained glass windows and handsome stalls for the Bishop, the Governor, Headmaster and staff.

As the school stands unprotected, practically on the sea shore, the sand is apt to sweep over and into the buildings, when the gales are high.

We saw the Big Hall, the Dining Hall, with very modern kitchens, the King's Court, a large quadrangle opened by the King and Queen in 1945, the Gymnasium with a stage for plays, the indoor swimming baths, the Art School and a well-equipped carpenter's shop.

The dormitories, each of which contains about sixteen or eighteen beds, are light and airy, and I was everywhere struck by the amount of light.

The cricket pitch and playing fields are open to the sea.

Above the centre of the college rises a high solid stone tower, which is not only a landmark for aeroplanes coming into the adjacent Ronaldsway airport, but can be seen for miles around.

There are 340 pupils, seventy of whom are day boys. The Headmaster told me that there were fifteen old boys at present in residence at Oxford, and I imagine a similar number at Cambridge.

The prefects, or prepositors, wear short gowns about the same size as Commoners' gowns at Oxford.

There is a healthy, happy atmosphere about the place which I very much liked.

The College was built in King William IV's reign, hence its name, in 1834, but was destroyed by fire ten years later. It was soon rebuilt, and the widow of Captain Quilliam, of H.M.S. *Victory* fame, gave to the chapel a handsome set of Communion Plate. The new Chapel was consecrated in 1879 and the old chapel is now the Library.

Between 1932 and 1940 the school was completely re-organised, reconstructed and enlarged owing to the efforts of an Old Boy, H. G. W. Hughes-Games, with the help of Tynwald.

The outstanding feature after the great tower is undoubtedly the Dining Hall, known as the Barrovian Hall, which has an unusually attractive series of coats of arms in the stained glass windows.

After leaving the College we paid a visit to Canon E. H. Stenning, the Vice-Principal, who, after forty-four years' devoted service, is reluctantly retiring. He will be a sad loss to the College, but he is a man of tremendous energy, and will continue to take an active part in the life of the Island. I found his book, *Isle of Man*, published by Robert Hale in the County Books Series, extraordinarily informative and entertaining.

I asked him about the report that I heard of two red squirrels reputed to have been seen recently in the Island. He said that there had been no squirrels for two thousand years, so he wasn't prepared to accept that rumour as true.

He told me of the prevalence of puffins on the Calf of Man, and also of the presence of choughs, as well as peregrines. He said that I ought to see the Manx sheep, of which only one flock is bred in Drummond's farm up in the hills near Snaefell. Apparently they tried to cultivate them on Langness, but whenever they were transported there, they found their way back to the hills, over a dozen miles away, in the dead of night, and no one ever saw them go.

We had luncheon in the café at the Airport, a light and ultra-modern restaurant, filled with passengers waiting to return to Renfrew.

As visibility was nil (we could scarcely see out of the windows) loudspeakers announced that passengers were requested to take the bus that was waiting to convey them to Jurby, from which airport it is always apparently possible to take off.

The Secretary came in to tell me how many thousand passengers had passed through the airport during the week-end. It was enough to convince me that travellers to the Island are rapidly becoming more air-minded. They come here not only from Ireland and Scotland and the more obvious English ports, but in increasing numbers from Newcastle-upon-Tyne.

After luncheon we drove to Rushen Abbey, where I found a surging mass of holiday-makers deposited from about a hundred motor coaches. They had come not only to sample the famous strawberries and cream, but to dance in a covered hall that stood in part of the old Abbey, in a manner of which Canon Stenning disapproved, and to wander round the magnificent garden, which is still bordered by the Abbey walls and contains not only strawberries and raspberries in profusion, but also a wonderful display of very colourful flowers.

Everywhere in the hedges the fuchsias and hydrangeas grew abundantly, and in the gardens I noticed particularly the sweet peas, roses and sweet williams.

There was a large crowd dancing Scottish reels and a bigger crowd standing round watching them.

Outside the gardens, which contain a Columbarium—the monks were not allowed to eat any meat except that of pigeons while travelling—we followed the peat-brown river up to the Monks' Bridge, built in 1134, a most picturesque narrow pack-horse bridge with mounting steps and a cobbled way.

Rushen Abbey was the last of the monasteries to survive the Dissolution. The old building, of which only the north transept tower remains, was originally cruciform. The Abbey walls were pulled down to make a house for the Deemster, which is now the Abbey Hotel. The property has been put to all sorts of uses, and today is partly a pleasure garden and partly a jam factory. The guest house is now used as a museum.

The Abbey stands on the site of a marsh, which the Cistercians drained by deepening the course of the Silverburn, which flowed through it.

At the Abbey ford stands the Abbey Mill, which still retains its mechanism, though the weir was destroyed by the great flood of 1930.

But, as Canon Stenning says, the outstanding feature of the whole place is not the over-popular pleasure garden (in spite of its flowers) but the Crossag or Monks' Bridge, with its hump back and two arches flanked by a wealth of trees.

"Whatever else," he says, "in the Isle of Man has to be omitted, everybody ought to go and see the Monks' Bridge."

After a return visit to Castle Rushen, which I have already described, we drove up the east coast to have tea at the Arragon Hotel, a converted country house with long sloping lawns just above the sea, a very bright, light house which contains a remarkable private collection of modern paintings and sculpture. I saw works by Paul Nash, Walter Sickert, Cézanne, Renoir and Henry Moore.

We did not go out after dinner as it was far too wet and it was blowing a gale. According to the radio this weather is universal.

TUESDAY

*The National Museum—
The Experimental Farm, Patrick—
Bishop's Court—Glen Helen*

The wind was fierce as ever but the rain let up periodically. We were taken at ten o'clock to see Sir Percy Cowley, the Deputy-Governor who, like everybody we have met in the Island, treated us with great affability and geniality.

Sir Percy has devoted his whole life to increasing the prestige and prosperity of the Island. He deplored the British tendency to spoon-feed everybody as having a deleterious effect on individual enterprise, and regretted that the Island has had to adopt the National Insurance scheme.

"The result is that it allows a man to do little or no work and to rely on the State to provide for him. I believe in the adage that if a man won't work neither shall he eat."

He told me that there were no political parties in the sense of Labour and Conservative. The Island is apparently pretty well conservative in spirit, with the agricultural interest predominant.

Politics are parochial. In one village arguments about Coronation celebrations became so heated that the Captain of the Parish in the end intervened with the comment:

"If you can't agree on what you want, there won't be a Coronation."

He agreed with the Speaker that the Island was singularly free from serious crime.

"I can only remember one murder in the whole of my life and that was when I was a very young man."

Up till two or three years ago the Island had been very rich, but there had been too much spending and they were now at the beginning of a period of severe retrenchment.

He said that the Manx Government were always on the

Niarbyl

Laxey Wheel

most cordial relations with the British Government, which gave the local government almost complete freedom in the management of their own affairs.

On leaving Sir Percy we went to the National Museum, where we had the great good fortune to find Mr. Ramsey Moore, at one time Attorney-General, just on the point of taking a party of visitors round. It is typical of the Island that a man of such high estate should give up his leisure to explain something of the treasures in which the Island is so rich. Everyone I have met is infused with this spirit of passionate devotion to the home of which they are so proud.

He began by making us sit round a relief plan of the Island on a large scale, and told us the legendary story of the origin of the Island. According to this there were once two giants, a giant of Cumberland and a giant of Ireland, who both fell in love with the same girl. They fought over her and the Irish giant won. As the Cumberland giant retreated towards his native hills, the Irish giant took a handful of Irish soil, now Lough Neagh, and threw it after his defeated opponent. It fell about half-way and is now the Isle of Man. Presumably Lough Neagh is the same size as the Island.

"The fact," said Mr. Moore, "is not very different from the legend. Only the giants were not men but natural forces."

"All the continent was joined together in the Ice Age. When the ice began to melt, there was a southward trend from the north and ice crushed the rock, depositing great hunks of granite and bringing down vast quantities of sandstone from Galloway, and even pieces of the rock of Ailsa Craig were deposited in Ayre."

Among other relics was an Irish elk, the complete skeleton of which was recovered from a bog. The skeleton still stands in the museum, complete even to its tail. Only the teeth were not original, these being cast from an elk in Ireland of the same period, 20,000 years ago. This skeleton has huge antlers, each horn having six points.

He showed us the fifteenth-century Sword of State, carried by the Governor at Tynwald, which is foreshortened because it was once lost and was found being used as a poker in a farmhouse.

We also saw the long staff which the Governor holds when he swears the oath to govern as uprightly as the staff he holds. As he reads his oath he is apt to let the staff incline from the vertical, which usually arouses amusement. As a contrast to this, the Deemster swears to be as balanced in his judgment as the backbone of a herring.

As we stood before the model of a Viking ship, he told us something of the history of the Island, how it was governed by the Norsemen from 900 till 1265, when it was ceded to Scotland after the Norse defeat at the Battle of Largs. It remained under the rule of Scotland for about a hundred years, and then England took it over and it was granted to the Stanleys in 1405, in the manner I have already sketched.

He explained how the sea had receded some eight feet in 2,000 years and that Douglas, as a result, was built on a raised beach.

In the earliest days a race of little people came over in coracles to fish and to hunt. He showed us the flints that were their earliest weapons, then the rounded stones that they made to form axes. Then he made a big jump to the Bronze Age, which led the Mediterranean people to search the northern seas for tin. Afterwards came the Megalithic people, who brought huge boulders of stone up to the hill-tops to form burial grounds. There are thirteen of these megalithic monuments in the Island.

We saw a case full of the armour, swords, blacksmith's

tools, etc., that were relics of a ship burial eight or nine hundred years ago.

And so we came to the magnificent Kermode collection of rubbings of the inscribed stones on which the whole story of Loki and Sigurd, and the Otter and Fafni, the King of the Dwarfs, was depicted. It is a grim story of the curse of gold, an Icelandic saga which Wagner used for his operas. On one particularly interesting stone there is a depiction on one side of Odin killing the wolf, and on the other side, the Christian cross, showing the change over in religion.

We then were shown a noteworthy memorial to T. E. Brown (1830-1897). This consists of a large niche, fronted by oak pillars, in front of a stained glass window, showing all the most famous characters about whom he wrote, with extracts from his poems inscribed in panels on the side walls. Mr. Ramsey Moore recited *Betsy Lee* very movingly.

We inspected a picture gallery devoted to the works of William Nicholson, William Hoggatt and Archibald Knox, nearly all landscapes of places in the island.

Then came a room full of stuffed birds, including a bittern, a white-tailed eagle, and a white starling.

Further on, we saw a completely furnished old cottage, over the door of which I noticed a cross made of rowan wood to keep out the evil spirits. Inside I saw a wide open hearth and the bread oven, together with the round dish covered with sheepskin on which the woman of the house baked her bread. There was the wooden trough in which the thick porridge was placed, and the bowls which were filled with milk and spoonfuls of porridge added. There were also lights in various forms, from rush lights to tallow candles.

I got the impression of a harsh, elemental existence in which time was of little object and work was continuous. A bedroom standing adjacent had little room for anything beyond the double bed, cradle and praying chair, but I did notice a cupboard let into the wall for clothes. The windows were very small and Mr. Ramsey Moore told us that these cottagers had a strong dislike of letting any air into their homes.

As we were going out I saw the wonderful silver Jurby chalice which dates from 1521.

This is one of the most worth-while museums I have ever visited, and gives a very thorough picture of the shape, history and customs of the Island.

In the afternoon, Mr. Faragher drove us past the Youth Hostel at Union Mills to Patrick, near Peel, where we inspected the Experimental Farm, which occupies the site of the German Prisoners of War camp of 1914-1918.

Some 20,000 or 30,000 prisoners were concentrated here on the slopes of the hill, on the summit of which is Corrin's Folly, where a man called Corrin decided to be buried.

There were large stone outbuildings, very modern in design, where I saw half a dozen of the largest and fattest bulls—Shorthorn, Friesian, Hereford and so on—that I have ever seen. We saw a herd of fine cows come in for milking, many litters of small pigs and some not so small. One sty was fitted with an infra-red lamp.

The Manx Government is nearing the end of a five-years' scheme to make cattle herds of the Island 100 per cent. tuberculin tested. Nearly five hundred herds, representing 10,000 cattle, have been tested and any diseased animals eradicated. The Government compensates the farmer for any cattle removed. The scheme started in 1949, and has reached the stage where there is a guarantee of pure milk for both visitors and residents. Apparently the farmers are co-operating whole-heartedly and when they want new stock, buy only attested animals. The scheme is in charge of the Government Veterinary Surgeon, Douglas Kerruish, who believes that once the Island becomes completely disease-free, it will not be difficult to keep it that way, since, on an island, complete control of imports can be exercised.

Away in the distance men were baling hay.

Experiments are also being made with various types of artificial manure and varieties of crops.

Altogether it struck me as a progressive and very go-ahead concern. It is being run by the Manx Agriculture and Fisheries Board, under the supervision of Mr. Howie.

We drove northward over the Glenfaba Bridge, which was the scene of an important event in Manx history, the Battle of Santwat. It appears that the battle was fought in the eleventh century between factions from the north and the south of the Island. The southerners were led by MacMarus, and the northerners by a Norse Earl named Outher. The tide of the battle went in favour of the northerners until the southern women, who were watching from the slopes of the valley, swept down to the assistance of their men and attacked with such fury that they threw the weight on the side of the southerners, who were the victors. A Manx tradition says that as a reward for their bravery, southern women were for centuries after given half their husbands' estate in widowhood, while the northern ladies received only a third.

The country in this vicinity is very pleasant. The Neb valley at this point is shady with trees and the river deep and placid. I continue to be surprised by the amazing variety of the Island's scenery.

It was pointed out to me that there were two types of mason-work in the building of Glenfaba Bridge. Right in the centre of the bridge it changed from one type to another. It seems that it dates from a period when each parish had its own highway authority and, since the river marks the boundary of the parishes of Patrick and German, each of these parishes built half the bridge. A triumph for local government! But the bridge is a very sound structure and a credit to both parishes.

We drove on by the west coast road to Glen Wyllin, a wide cleft or ravine which has been laid out as a pleasure garden with fine grass lawn tennis courts, a pool for motor boats, recreation ground for children and a huge café, where we had tea.

I saw a tremendous number of small children. The Isle of Man natives have a pleasant habit of asking over poor children from Liverpool and other big cities, and giving them a holiday in these places. These children were certainly enjoying themselves.

We went on to Bishop's Court to call on the Bishop of Sodor and Man, who took us all over the palace, parts of which date back to Norse times. He showed us a book kept by Bishop Wilson, who lived to be ninety-three, and was Bishop here at the end of the seventeenth century and beginning of the eighteenth. He was responsible for the production of the first book ever to be written in the Manx language (about 1700) and a Prayer Book written in Manx and English.

Many pieces of Bishop Wilson's furniture still remain in the Palace, including his chair, desk and tables. From the Drawing Room window we got a fine view of sloping lawns rose gardens and the mountains rising behind.

We also saw the Bishop's Private Chapel, the Pro-Cathedral of the Diocese, and were then taken by his Domestic Chaplain along the avenue known as the Twelve Apostles, past a stream, to the immense garden, with long herbaceous borders and a plantation of giant raspberries, on which we feasted.

He then took us up the Bishop's private glen, full of tall trees, and containing the mast of the *Belle Isle*, which surmounts a mound among the trees.

There is also a stone and two old cannon. The stone

bears an inscription stating that the mound was formed and called Mount Aeolus by Bishop Hildesley, to commemorate a victory of the English over the French on February 28th, 1780. The two cannon are trophies of the victory. The battle was fought off the north coast of the Island between English and French squadrons, and the guns could be heard at Bishop's Court. It was a resounding victory for the British. The *Belle Isle*, a frigate of 44 guns, was captured, and her captain (who commanded the squadron), Francois Thurot, killed. Thurot had been very successful in preying on English merchant ships. After the battle the ships put into Ramsey Bay.

Up and down this path Bishops have perambulated, preparing their addresses from time immemorial.

It is like all the Manx glens, a wild and lovely place of water, thick undergrowth and tall trees.

We saw another mound on the return journey—about a mile north of Kirk Michael Village. It was called Cronk-y-Croghee which, I was told, means 'Hill of Hanging'. A picturesque name ! It seems that it was the place of execution for capital offences in ecclesiastical law.

At Cronk Urleigh on the other side of Kirk Michael village we saw the hill which was pointed out as the meeting place of the Tynwald in the fifteenth century. An old Statute Book recorded an insurrection there in 1422. The Lieutenant-Governor and his men appear to have been driven from the hill by the rebels and to have fled to Kirk Michael, where they took refuge in the parish church. They must have run about two miles. The ringleaders of the rising were drastically dealt with. They were charged with misusing the Lieutenant-Governor, Henry Byron, and his men in Michael Church, and sentenced to be drawn behind wild horses, beheaded and quartered. Byron was the Governor for Sir John Stanley.

We made a detour at Baare garroo to see Spooyt

Vane Glen. Running through narrow lanes with banked hedges we passed a very small mission hall and small, quaint, old cottages. From there we had to walk over a cart track for a quarter of a mile before suddenly finding the glen lying before us. We were about 300 feet up on the bank with the most beautiful wooded glen beneath us. There is a fine waterfall at the top which drops over one hundred feet. There is a small building which was called the Priests House. A priest was said to have lived there and to have fallen over the waterfall when on his way to evening prayer.

Spooyt Vane is very secluded and I imagine few visitors to the Isle of Man see it.

The lane we had been following comes out on the coast route. I saw a big quartz stone standing in a field which served for years as a sundial. When the sun struck it in a certain way the people on the farm knew it was noon.

We drove to Glen Helen, which is the only inland glen and one of the largest. It contains at its entrance a hotel, a large dance hall which is very popular, and a Swiss café. We walked for about a couple of miles up this glen, which has a fine river tumbling over boulders and large waterfalls coming down the mountain-side.

There are paths running along both sides, but the bridges are few and far between. There is one at the bottom, and another about two miles up, which we crossed. The track is rather rough and on this day was full of puddles, but the trees are quite beautiful and the steep banks covered with bracken. One could spend many profitable days doing nothing beyond exploring these glens, in which the Island is very rich.

A recent flood had carried down one mighty tree and left its traces all up the length of the glen, which is protected from all the winds, and shady the whole way up.

This glen reminded me of the valleys of the East and

West Lyn above Watersmeet, but it struck me as even wilder, the gorge deeper and the trees more prolific.

It was a delightful walk, the most rewarding of its kind of any that I have taken in the Island.

There is a movement on foot for the Government to acquire all the glens and open them to the public free of charge. At present some are free and others are private property, where small fees are imposed.

Glen Helen is particularly popular at nights by reason of the concerts that are held in the hall, as well as dances. As it only takes about twenty minutes from Douglas, it is a convenient distance for visitors to reach. But the wise visitor is he who comes in the day-time and gives himself time to explore the whole of the glen, which penetrates for several miles right into the heart of the mountains.

WEDNESDAY   *The Nunnery—St. John's*
                                Cattle Mart—Foxdale Mines

A very high wind for about the twelfth day running. It never seems to let up in the Island, and it blows viciously and with great force everywhere.

Mr. Faragher called for us and took us first to the Nunnery, originally founded in honour of St. Bridget.

It is an enormous grey stone country house enclosed in woods, within a stone's throw of Douglas. It was here that Peter Heywood, of the Mutiny on the *Bounty* fame, was born, as well as his sister, Nessy, who made an epic journey to plead for his life to Queen Anne. In 1780 the estate was sold to John Taubman, whose son-in-law, General Goldie, pulled down the old house and rebuilt the present one, which is now the home of Captain Fry-Goldie-Taubman. Of the original buildings only the chapel remains and we were taken first to see this. It was wonderfully restored by Leigh Goldie-Taubman in 1887. Above the gateway is the

Angelus bell, and I saw two peacocks in the precincts, on one wall of which are two handsome crucifixes, one studded with precious jewels.

In view of the many fine paintings and carved figures, mainly of Italian origin, that enrich this little church, it seems a great pity that it is no longer used for public worship, as it was in Mr. Faragher's youth, when he was a member of the choir. In these days, however, it is easy to see that the stipend of a private chaplain and the expense of keeping open a private chapel are one of those luxuries that practically no landowner can afford. It is some consolation to know that there is no danger of this very interesting chapel being neglected.

Some people claim that St. Bridget was not only the patroness but actually founded the nunnery and became its first Prioress. In medieval times the Prioress was a baroness in her own right and held jurisdiction over both the spiritual and temporal courts.

In the twelfth century the monks of Rushen Abbey temporarily established themselves in Douglas and we hear of a Cistercian Abbey of St. Mary de Douglas. In 1313, Robert the Bruce after landing at Ramsey spent a night here. But in the fifteenth and sixteenth centuries there was always a Prioress, which means that the buildings had obviously reverted to their original owners.

When the Nunnery was dissolved in 1540, the then Prioress, Margaret Goodman, was not only allowed to go free with her three nuns, but she actually married Robert Calcott, the Lord's Comptroller of the Island.

The Earl of Mann, to whom the estate reverted, sold the Nunnery ruins, after the buildings had been pulled down, to his Comptroller, and with the stones Calcott built a new mansion for his ex-Prioress wife. Later the estate was sold to the Heywood family, who again rebuilt the house.

The eighteenth-century building that I saw stands

impressively with a broad front and big windows high on a terrace, overlooking several acres of lawns and practically encircled by trees.

The butler, who was conducting us, then took us up some stone spiral steps into the Dining Hall, the walls of which are hung with portraits of the present owner and several of his forbears.   One of these was by Sargent.

I was surprised to see a portrait of Anne Boleyn, but the butler was unable to tell us anything about her connection with the family.

He then delivered us into the hands of the head gardener, who took us through a series of hot-houses full of peaches, melons, tomatoes and grapes as well as a great variety of exotic flowers and shrubs.   One plant in particular excited us all as we had never seen anything like it.   As soon as the gardener touched a leaf the whole plant shrank, all the leaves folded up and temporarily seemed to wither.

"We call that," he said, "the Sensitive or Tender plant. It soon recovers."

The greater part of the produce from the immense gardens and hot-houses is sold locally.

Beyond the garden we came to the glass-roofed Winter Garden, with many steps leading round rockeries, and a splendid display of bougainvillea, oleander, camellias and other vividly coloured flowers that one associates with the Mediterranean coast.

As we left the grounds, we passed a tall obelisk erected to the memory of Brigadier-General Thomas Leigh-Goldie, who was killed at the battle of Inkerman.

On the way to our next port of call, Mr. Faragher, who is a mine of information, told me more of the history of the Fort Anne Hotel, in which we were staying.

At one time, Fort Anne became the home of Sir William Hillary, the founder of the Royal National Life-Boat Institution.

On one occasion Sir William went out in a life-boat to rescue the crew of the packet boat, *St. George*, which was driven by a storm between the Conister and Pollack rocks in Douglas Bay, and wrecked. Twenty-two of the passengers and crew were saved, but Sir William was seriously injured after being washed overboard and crushed between the life-boat and the wreck.

It was this disaster that led to the building of 'the Tower of Refuge' which was erected on the Conister Rock in 1843 at a cost of £255 which, in view of its rather grand castellated appearance seems extraordinarily little.

In common, I imagine, with the majority of other visitors I had taken it for granted that this picturesque landmark, which stands out in the Bay at no great distance from the harbour, was a Napoleonic or even perhaps Tudor fort. It never occurred to me, until Mr. Faragher enlightened me, that it was built to mark the dangerous low rocks, and to provide a sanctuary for shipwrecked sailors. At low tide most of the rock is exposed and crowds of visitors row out to explore the Tower.

One curious fact about it sticks in my memory. The designer, John Welch, had a partner called Hansom, who became world-famous as the designer of the 'Hansom' cab.

After leaving the Nunnery, Mr. Faragher drove us across the Island along the Peel road, turning north at St. John's to visit Moore's Tweed Mills, which lie hidden at the foot of a very picturesque wooded glen.

For many centuries Manx woollen and linen fabrics have been famous. They weave a plaid but, unlike the Scottish plaid, it is not chequered. There are no Manx tartans. I had seen in the Museum and in several cottages the old spinning wheels and hand looms. As well as the wool, flax was spun and linen made in the Island in the seventeenth century and onwards. At the beginning of the nineteenth century about 60,000 yards of linen cloth was exported annually. Then came the era of the woollen mills, using water power, and very fine Manx tweed cloth was manufactured. To-day, the steam engine has largely superseded water power and the yarn is mainly imported from Britain.

The present owner of the St. John's Mill, Mr. Moore, is the great-grandson of the founder of the mill, which was opened in 1840.

I was surprised by the size of the mill, and by the variety and quality of the woollen materials that I watched being manufactured. I have visited scores of woollen mills and this one struck me as being one of the most efficient and up to date. Particularly was I struck by the absence of fuss as I went from the sorting to the scouring, from the dyeing to the weaving, and as I watched one quiet woman in command of three hundred and twenty spindles on one machine. I saw men sorting out the clippings of wool that had been imported from Ireland, Scotland and elsewhere. They do this all by hand to test the various grades and qualities.

I was shown two boilers that had started work at a cable station in Douglas as far back as 1896, and were still going strong.

Mr. Moore also showed me the elaborate precautions that are taken to prevent, as far as possible, any pollution of the Island streams. But I was most interested, naturally, in inspecting the rolls of finished tweed cloth, which appeared to be as durable as any Highland tweed and there was a most pleasing variety of colour and thickness.

I was considerably surprised to learn that eighty per cent. of this mill's products go direct to the United States.

I certainly intend to have my next suit made up from Mr. Moore's Manx tweed.

From this mill we went to St. John's cattle mart.

There wasn't much going on in the mart as the three auctioneers were mainly occupied in seeing the beasts weighed and allocating them to the butchers at what someone said was the government-controlled price of 1s. 1d. per lb. Sitting on the raised benches of the mart, above the arena, were about half a dozen grizzled farmers and butchers, three of whom were wearing large ear-rings.

By a piece of singular good fortune a well-known farmer in the Island, Mr. Brownsdon, was in the market. He is the only man still to breed a flock of pure Manx sheep. He described his flock with loving care.

"The ram," he said, "has four long re-curved horns and is a grand-looking animal, with a reddish-brown fleece, which was always used to make the Manx homespun cloth, usually worn undyed, and almost impossible to wear out. The ewe, by the way, has only two rather shorter horns. The Loghtan sheep, as we call it, is lean to look at, with a high back and is not unlike a goat. It has all the agility and activity of a goat. The breeds that we farmers find most suited to our Island conditions are Kerry Hill crossed with Border Leicesters, and the Scots black-faced. We do well enough with sheep to be able to export them. On the other hand, we still have to import beef, though we have enough surplus of pigs to be able to export half of them."

This statement puzzled me as I had seen in my wanderings what struck me as a prodigious number of well-cared for cattle.

I must have mistaken quality for quantity. There are about 25,000 cattle and about 65,000 sheep in the Island.

It is, of course, quite a problem feeding half a million extra visitors in the summer months, and this doubtless accounts for the importation of the beef.

My visit to the Island was just a little early for the Agricultural shows. There are two, usually held within a week of each other. Judging by the stock I have seen they must be quite impressive. Part of the show consists of horse-riding events, which are very popular. One of these shows is held in alternate years at the Nunnery estate and at Ramsey. The other is held at Castletown and is organised by the Southside farmers.

In the Douglas Hotel in front of the market we found visitors from Liverpool drinking the export ale and discussing the succulent taste of the Island speciality, scallops, which are called tanrogans.

This hotel was built as a residence for one of the Dukes of Atholl, and dates from about 1780. A much more imposing edifice, built by John, the fourth Duke of Atholl in 1800, is now the Castle Mona Hotel in the centre of the promenade in Douglas. It was said to have cost £40,000 to build, which must have been a prodigious sum in those days. It was the only property in the Island which was not sold to the British Government by the Duke in 1825, when he finally disposed of all his rights in the Island.

It appears that the Villa Marina, with its handsome ball-room and gardens, was also built as a private residence, although it shows little signs of it now. It was the residence of Henry Noble, a great benefactor to Douglas, and was acquired and converted by the Douglas Corporation.

After indulging in some badinage with the landlady in his native Manx ("We all know how to salute each other in Manx"), Mr. Faragher drove us on to the derelict mines of Foxdale, where rows of roofless cottages, broken-down chimneys, a large dam and scarred earth are all that remain to remind us of a once great industry.

"This lead mining," said Mr. Faragher, "is one of the oldest of our industries. I know that as far back as the thirteenth century the monks were given the free use of all kinds of mines, with full profits."

These Foxdale mines came into prominence in the early part of the nineteenth century, when a new vein was discovered which yielded about 2,500 tons every year. The output kept on rising till 1875, when 12,000 tons of ore were produced.

Lead's best year was in 1892, when nearly 7,000 tons were mined.

These Foxdale mines are cuttings into one lode which runs east and west, and is cut right across by the Foxdale stream, which exposed the original lode. Thirteen shafts were sunk along a line of about two and a half miles. The most westerly shaft is Beckwith's, which was sunk to a depth of over a thousand feet and about five hundred feet below sea level. This yielded 50,000 tons of ore.

The mine beside the main road had four shafts with underground cross-galleries, and went down to a depth of 2,000 feet. This was the last to close down, in 1910.

"There is another shaft about a mile off the road, which is of particular interest to me, as it was known as Faragher's," said Mr. Faragher, "though I never made a profit out of it. And I don't believe anybody else did, either."

"This mine had two other names as well as Faragher's. Some called it 'Hodgson's' and others the 'Louisa'. It was the last of the sinkings, and started well, but was soon proved unproductive. The most profitable group of workings were those in Foxdale village. In one year they extracted nearly 5,000 tons of lead ore, which contained £40,000 worth of silver.

"Just east of the Eary dam there were three more shafts sunk to a level of nearly 1,000 feet, but here the main lode seems to have come to an end and a vast amount of money was lost."

"As a matter of fact," I said, "the sight of these derelict stacks, roofless miners' cottages and masses of scree and rubble, are quite familiar to me. They remind me of my boyhood. I was brought up in a Derbyshire village in the hills near a lot of lead-mines that had first been worked by the Romans, and quite a few prospectors settled in my father's parish, sunk shaft after shaft and all of them lost their capital. It was a sort of craze, like gambling on football pools."

"With rather more at stake," said Mr. Faragher. "It's an expensive job sinking shafts, putting up machinery, hiring labour, and all for nothing."

"The curious thing was that all these prospectors seem, as far as I can remember them, to have been hard-headed, experienced mining engineers, but they were incurable optimists. They always thought that they would strike lead just round the corner, a few yards further on, and nothing would induce them to stop until they were face to face with ruin."

"I expect that the Romans had pretty well curry-combed your hills," said Mr. Faragher.

"Well, I've explored mile after mile of their corridors and caverns. I suppose they could afford to go on and on indefinitely with their slave labour. They didn't clean up altogether, because Wirksworth became a tremendously important centre for lead-mining right up to the nineteenth century and, in point of fact, the Long Rake mine at Darley Dale still produces eighty per cent of all the lead mined in Great Britain."

"We seem to have stopped quarrying limestone," said Mr. Faragher, "but we owe the wonderful surface of the Manx roads entirely to the granite quarries at Santon and Dhoon. There are still a few quarries supplying shale for building walls, but we've stopped producing our famous slate 'beams'. They burn the limestone at Malew to supply lime for the fields and building, and at Peel they make a good serviceable brick from disintegrated slate. Of course, we're rich in sand and gravel, as you've seen, and we use that, with imported cement, to build modern houses. As a matter of fact, this particular area is rich in Fuller's Earth, but that industry has been killed by cheap imports."

He drove onwards over the 'Plains of Heaven', a very pleasant open country, bequeathed to the Douglas Corporation by the owner, from which there is a superb view right over the town and whole of the bay.

In the other direction we looked over the gently sloping Marown Valley towards Greeba Castle. Some people say that the Victorian artist, John Martin, made the sketches for a painting on the shoulder of the hill on which we stood.

He called the painting the Plains of Heaven, and gave the place the name which has stuck to it. It is very apt. There has been a revival of interest in John Martin's works recently, and an exhibition in the Whitechapel Art Gallery included the 10ft. by 6ft. canvas, "The Plains of Heaven". Martin was a frequent visitor to the Island and married a Douglas woman.

Mr. Faragher said that the farmland in the Douglas direction was called Dreamland. It is an Island of picturesque names. In this case it seems to have come from a Manx name, Dreemlang. There is a remarkable echo here. If the wind is blowing from the south, words come back from the mountains across the valley very distinctly.

In one of the fields is a monument which has been preserved by the National Trust. It is called St. Patrick's Chair. It consists of large boulders, one with a cross carved on it. They form a platform on which St. Patrick is traditionally said to have sat to preach to the people on the slope below. If you sit on the chair and repeat the Lord's Prayer you will never be lonely.

On the way, Mr. Faragher regaled me with fascinating stories of Manx folk-lore.

Mr. Bond and others had told me of the *buggane* who

unroofed the little church of St. Trinian's at Marown every time they tried to put the roof on, so that in the end it was left unroofed, as it is now.   What I had not realised before was that the *buggane* was not, as I thought, a pixie, but a malevolent giant with a terrifying voice that he reserves for stormy nights.   He spends a large part of his time unroofing buildings.   In an Island of mighty winds, this ought not to be difficult.

There was a *buggane* on Slieuwhallian, the mountain down which they used to roll the witches in barrels, and another at Kirk Maughold.

Unlike the 'little people', the giants were always inimical to man.   The 'little people' could be mischievous, and children, as I heard for myself at the Fairies' Bridge at Ballaglonney, are very polite in their salutation to them, but their reputation is not wholly bad.   They can be beneficent, they can be malicious, just as the pixies. Housewives still leave scraps of food or a dish of milk for them outside their doors, and no deserted house is ever pulled down lest the 'little people' should be homeless.

There are two sorts of 'little people', the *glashtan* and the *phynnodderee*, and one of these is much more mischievous than the other, haunting lonely places to frighten women and children, turning milk sour, making chimneys smoke, and causing all kinds of unpleasant accidents.

Quite a number of people told me stories of the 'little people', but I can't remember who told me about the fairy cup of Ballafletcher, which I saw in the Museum. It is made of glass and is rather like a tumbler, but very heavy and richly decorated.   It is just over four inches high. This cup had a fairy guardian called a Lhiannan-shee. The idea was that so long as the cup was safely kept, the fairy would keep its owner in peace and plenty but, if it was broken or ill-used, then the owner would be ruined.

It is said to have originally belonged to St. Olaf in the very dim and distant past and being of exceptional beauty was placed in his shrine. It was stolen from there by his successor Magnus, King of Norway about the year 1100, and after that there is no record of it for several centuries. But it was in the possession of the Fletchers of Kirk Braddan at the end of the sixteenth century, and apparently placed in the charge of the church and used by the Bishop. When the Fletcher family died out in 1778, it was acquired by the Caesar family and kept at Seafield, where it was brought out only at the high festivals of Christmas and Easter, when it was filled with wine and the head of the family had to drink at one draught the whole cupful in honour of the fairy guardian.

There seems to be a link between wine cups and fairies.

In view of the Island's close historic association with Scandinavia, I was surprised not to hear more people refer to *trolls*, which seemed to infest almost every mountain in Norway. Except for the place-name Trollaby, which means the home of the *trolls*, I heard scarcely any reference to them. Perhaps they have merged into the *bugganes*.

On the other hand I heard talk of the *cughtagh*, the sea-monster, whose breathing can be heard in the sea-caves on the calmest days and his strident voice in stormy weather, but who never appears owing to his shyness and dislike of human beings. And as you would expect in an Island whose rocks are so frequently patronised by seals there are plenty of stories of mermaids seen combing their hair and luring their human lovers to treasure-filled palaces under the sea.

And as a male counterpart to the mermaids, I heard tell of the water-bull, called by the Manx *gabbyl-ushtey*, a quite friendly beast who invited men as well as women to ride on his back, and then disappeared with them into the sea.

This is, of course, the Manx version of the Europa and Zeus legend.

Considering how strong a hold so many of their ancient superstitions still exert on the Islanders, I was surprised to find how few of the old folk-customs are still observed. One of the most interesting is the 'Hunting of the Wren' on St. Stephen's Day.

Groups of boys then go from house to house in procession carrying a small basket decorated with feathers. It is constructed of two wooden hoops, tied at right-angles, festooned with ribbons and paper streamers and containing a decorated cushion.

They then sing an odd ditty, which appears to go on interminably.

It begins :—

"We'll away to the wood, says Robin to Bobbin,
    We'll away to the wood, says Dickin to Robin,
We'll away to the wood, says Jack o' the land,
    We'll away to the wood, says everyone."

It goes on to describe the hunt and killing of the wren and ends "He's ate, he's ate, says Robin to Bobbin."

Originally a wren was hunted, killed and then plucked, the feathers being sold as charms.

To-day, the ceremony is carried out bloodlessly, with the substitution of a dummy of feathers.

Nobody seems to know the origin of this curious custom, but some say that it is a relic of an old Miracle Play, celebrating the stoning of St. Stephen. Another suggestion is that the wren impersonated a witch or wicked fairy, who would regain her original form if she was allowed to live till New Year's Day.

What is noteworthy is the fact that the wren keeps on cropping up in folk lore in many countries and is often looked on as a bird of great sanctity.

What strikes me as incongruous is the fact that a bird who is held in such veneration for the rest of the year should be sacrificed at Christmas.

There was observed until fairly recently the custom of driving all cattle into the 'farm-street' on May Day Eve, for that was the night when the initiation of witches took place, and primroses, kingcups and other yellow flowers were put round the house to avert the evil eye, and the gorse and other bushes and hedges round the fields were set on fire to protect the fields from the witches' eyes.

The islander's belief in witches is deep-rooted and not, I believe, wholly eradicated even now, which is scarcely surprising in view of the power of the witches' curse. Apparently, the witches used to go quite openly to the houses they selected for their ill-wishing. Carrying a broom, the witch would sweep the dust toward the house and then curse in detail the bed and board, flocks and herds, children and property, and everything connected with the hapless family. When one thinks of the terror they caused and power that they wielded over the credulous and simple-minded, it isn't surprising that pretty drastic measures were taken to put a stop to their activities.

Doing penance with sheet and candle at different churches may not have deterred the more evil-minded, but imprisonment in the dungeon at Peel, the ducking stool, being thrown into the water or rolled down the hill in a barrel studded with nails, ought to have helped to reduce their numbers.

As an antidote or counterblast to the witches were the witch-doctors, herbalists who were often able to undo much of the harm caused by the witches. The most famous of these was Teare, who lived in Kirk Andreas, but had clients all over the island. Everyone had implicit faith in his curative powers. He didn't worry overmuch about human ailments, but he had prodigious success with animals and crops. He claimed to have inside knowledge of the way the witches worked and of the cures for their evil practices.

He had a special garden of herbs which were reputed to possess anti-witch properties and this garden became so famous that it was almost destroyed by fishermen who used to enter it by night and roll on it in the hope of being touched by some of the plants that would avert misfortune. Plants that possess special healing properties include dandelion, goutweed, St. John's wort and ribwort.

THURSDAY *We depart*

On Thursday, July 23rd, we sailed for home, again on the *King Orry*, with a fair following wind and a moderate sea. We left the Island with many regrets. We had made many friends and found courtesy, kindness and generous hospitality everywhere.

The invigorating air added enormously to our enjoyment of a scene that, in Douglas, was always gay and cheerful, and the Island was full of delightful surprises. I had often visited it before, but never fully realised how extraordinarily wide is its appeal.

The archaeologist finds in it an inexhaustible treasure house, for there seem to be no end to the incised stones and crosses and the very ancient circles and burial grounds. For those who are interested in the customs and folk-lore of the Norsemen it provides a prolific and profitable hunting ground, and great care has been taken by native scholars and antiquaries to preserve as much evidence as possible of the old order of things in language, clothes, tools and way of living throughout the centuries.

Mingled with this respect for the past is every aid to enjoyment of the present.

Every effort has been made to see that visitors can get

the best possible fishing, the most enjoyable, safest bathing and the most sporting golf.

From my own particular point of view I like the Isle of Man best for its great variety of scenery.

The number of glens which, in some ways, resemble the chines of the Isle of Wight, on a far larger scale of course, is bewildering. They are full of beauty and make ideal walking for those who like the presence of water and the shade of trees.

Then there are the coastal cliffs, as magnificent as those in Cornwall, but for some reason much less widely known. Everywhere there are the rounded high hills, notably South Barrule, all extremely easy of access and providing superb views over the sea towards the hills of England, Scotland, Wales and Ireland.

It is a large enough island for the walker to find absolute quietude as well as unspoilt beauty in all his wanderings and, when he feels gregarious at night time, he can find tip-top entertainment of every sort in Douglas.

It is worth noticing that north-country families have, for generations, gone back to the Island every summer for their annual holiday. It is a commonplace that the Northerner has an unerring instinct for what is good.

Now that the excellent air service has made the Island so much more easily accessible to everyone, I can see more and more families from the South discovering the allurement of what, I think, can fairly claim to be the liveliest and most progressive island round our coast.

INDEX

Aeolus, Mount, 135
Agriculture and Fisheries, Board of, 106, 133
Ailsa Craig, 129
Albert, Prince Consort, 21, 71
Alexander III, King of Scotland, 35-6
Alexandra, Queen, 104
Andreas, 94
Angling Festival, 118
Anne, Queen, 137
Arbory, 61-2
Archaeological Society, 21
Arderry, 65
Atholl, Dukes of, 48, 61, 71, 105, 143
Aufrica, Princess of Mann, 74
Auldyn, Glen, 82
Ayre, Point of, 21, 93-4

Baase Illian Dhone, 48
Bacon, 68
Baldwin, 64-5
Ballabeg, 62
Ballachurry, 96
Balladoole, 53-4
Ballafletcher, 147
Ballafreer, 76-7
Ballaglass, 20, 90, 114
Ballaglonney, 147
Ballaratcliffe, 95
Ballasalla, 62
Ballaugh, 66, 108-9
Ballure, 82
Bangor & Saul, Monastery of, 74
Barrow, Bishop, 48
Barrule, South, 59, 72-3, 76, 110-11, 152
Beckwith's shaft, 144
Beinn-y-Phott, 70
Belfast, 12, 38, 89, *et passim*
Bella Cashtal, 38
Belle Isle, 134-5
Bellelby Farm, 73
Betham, William, 71
Bird Sanctuary, 17
Biological Station, Port Erin, 86
Birmingham, 9, 38
Bishop's Court, 134
Blackpool, 31, 38
Bligh, Captain, 71
Boleyn, Anne, 139
Bonaparte, Napoleon, 49, 108, 123
Bounty, The, 71, 137
Bradda Head, 43, 54, 60, 86, 87
Braddan, 68, 99
Braddan Bridge, 107
Bragg, Sir W., 124
Bray Hill, 109
Bride village, 94
Brown, Rev. R., 107
Brown, T. E., 107, 124, 131
Bruce, Robert the, 36-8, 62, 138
Bungalow, The, 70, 97, 114-15
Bushels House, 58
Byron, Henry (Lieut.-Governor), 135

Caesar family, 148
Caine, Hall, 13, 14, 80, 101
Calcott, Robert, 138
Calf of Man, 17, 18, 45, 55 *et seq.*, 73, 86, 101, 121, 125
Carey, George, 58
Carraghyn, 64
Carrick, 110
Cashen, William, 74
Cashtel-yn-Ard, 21
Castletown, 38, 47, 48 *et seq.*, 55, 61, 72, 74, 111, 116, 121, 143
Cattle Mart (St. John's), 141-2
Chalenor, James, 47
Charles I, King, 43 *et seq.*
Charles II, King, 45, 47 *et seq.*
Chasms, The, 56
Chickens Rock Light, 58
Christian, Edward, 42 *et seq.*
Christian, Ewan, 97
Christian, Fletcher, 71, 97
Christian, Phillip, 105
Christian, William, 45 *et seq.*, 97
Circle of Mull, 59
Circle of the Hill, 37
Cistercian order, 25, 48, 127, 138
Claddagh Common, 68
Clegg, Mrs., 75
Cleveland, Ohio, 27
Clothworkers, School of, Peel, 105
Cloven Stones, 89
Codrun's Folly, 132
Colby, 60 *et seq.*
Courcy, John de, Lord of Ulster, 74
Constitution of Tynwald, 37
Corbould, Henry, R.A., 70
Cornaa, 90
Corony Hill, 91
Cowley, Sir Percy, 128
Cregeen, Archibald, 60 *et seq.*
Cregneish, 55, 57, 95
Cromwell, Oliver, 44 *et seq.*
Cronk-ny-Irey-Lhaa, 87
Cronk-y-Croghee, 135
Cronk Urleigh, 135
Cronk-y-Voddy, 135
Crosby, 76
Crossag, 127
Crovan, Godred, 82, 103
Crovan, Lagman, 82
Crovan, Olaf, 82, 103
Crow, Captain Hugh, 81
Cunliffe-Owen, Mrs., 81, 108, 114
Curragh, The, 67, 94
Curtis Herring Factory, 101

Dalby, 73-4
Dee, Dr. John, 51
Deemster, The, 14, 101
Deemsters, 14, 32, 37, 41, 42 *et seq.*
Deemster's Cairn, 65
Derby, Charlotte, Countess of, 45 *et seq.*

Derby, Earls of, 34, 39, 96, 103, 112
Derbyhaven, 112
Derby House, 39
Dhu, River, 17
Dhoon, Glen, 90, 114, 145
Douglas, 10, 17, 22, 26, 30, 47, 54, 60, 64–5, 70, 115,
     et passim
Dreamland, 146
Drink, Glen, 90
Druidale, 66
Druids, The, 62
Drummond's Bank, 65
Drummond's Farm, 125
Drumskerry, 114
Drury, Rev. William, 78
Dublin, 12, 35, 38, 82 97
Duckenfield, Colonel, 46
Duke, Geoff., 109
Dumfries, 21, 110
Dundas, Sir Ambrose, 26
Dunure, 116

Eary dam, 144
Edmund (son of Henry III), 35–6
Edward VIII, King, 104
Elizabeth I, Queen, 41, 42, 51, 58
Eyre, 126
Eyreton Castle, 76

Fairfax, Lord, 47
Fairies' Bridge, 112, 147
Falcons, order of, 81
Faragher's Shaft, 144
Farrar, Dean, 124
Fenella (locomotive), 116
Fenella's Leap, 102, 104
Fletcher family, 148
Forbes, Prof. Edward, 66
Fort Anne, 13, 24
Fowler, Thomas, 124
Foxdale, 76, 143–4
Freemasons, 52
Fry, Lieutenant, 19
Fry-Goldie-Taubman family, 13, 19, 108, 137

Garrett of Sulby, William, 43
Garwick, 89 *et seq.*
Galloway, 110, 129
George V, King, 91
George VI, King, 124
Geological Society, 66
German, parish of, 133
Glasgow, 38, 116
Ginger Hill, 109
Glass, River, 17, 64
Glenfaba, 37, 133
Glen Helen, 136–7
Godredson, Olaf, 36
Goodman, Margaret, 138
Gooseneck, 109
Governor's Bridge, 110
Great Wall, The, 69
Greeba Bridge, 109
Greeba Castle, 146
Guthrie, Jimmy, 22

Hague Farmhouse, 71
Hango Hill, 47
Hansom, 140
Harald, King, 36
Helena Harris, 102
Henry III, King, 35
Henry VIII, King, 48
Heywood, Nessy, 137
Heywood, Peter, 71, 137
Heywood, Robert, 111
Highland Park Cemetery, 27
Hillary, Sir William, 139
Hill of Hanging, 135
Hill of The Rising Sun, 73, 87
Hill of The Watch, 73
Hildesly, Bishop, 135
Hipkins, Mathew, 52
Hodgson's shaft, 144
Hoggatt, William, 131
Horse Leap, The, 117

Injebreck, 64
Irish Rebellion, 72
Isabella, The Lady, 20, 114
Isle of Man Examiner, 27

Jurby, 94 *et seq.*, 122, 126, 132

Karran, Richard, 83
Keeil-y-Chirrn, 73
Kelly, The Giant, 80
Kelly, Harry, 57
Kennish, Wm., 91
Kentraugh, 54
Keristal, 118
Kermode Collection, The, 131
Kermode, P. M. C., 81
Kerruish, Douglas, 132
Keys, House of, 14, 15, 32, 41, 42, 44, 47 *et passim.*
Killabane, 64
King William's College, 38, 47, 111, 123 *et seq.*
Kinvig, 31
Kirby Park, 108
Kirk Andreas, 150
Kirk Braddan, 13, 33, 64, 78, 107, 148
Kirkmichael, 108–9, 113, 135
Kirk Maughold, 147
Kissack (locomotive), 116
Kitterland, 59
Knox, Archibald, 131
Kremlin, 16

Langness, 111
Langness Lighthouse, 112, 118, 125
Largs, Battle of, 130
Laurel Bank, 109
Laxey, 19, 20, 21, 70, 89 *et seq.*, 114 *et seq.*
Legislative Council, 14, 32
Leigh-Goldie, Brig.-Gen. T., 137, 139
Leon, Jack, 25, 28
Lezayre, 68, 97

Lifeboat Institution, Royal National, 139
Lily, brig, 59
Liverpool, 9, 12, 13, 31, 38, 59, 105, 134, 143, *et passim*
Lloyds', 59
Loch, Lieutenant-Governor, 74
Lonan, 89
Louisa's shaft, 144
Lynam, 'Skipper', 124

MacMarus, 133
Magnus, King of Norway, 148
Malew, 145
Man, Bishop of, 41
Man, Earl of, 138
Man, Kings of, 39, 40, 42, 103
Man, Lords of, 36, 40, 41, 48, 103
Manchester, 25, 31, 38
Manx dictionary, 60
Manx Cat, 18
Manx Fencibles, 72
Manx hen, 19
Manx language, 15, 17, 25, 27, 33, *et passim*
Manx Mercury, 51
Manx sheep, 142
Marine Parade, 118
Maroun, 15, 146, 147
Martin, John, 146
Mary, Queen, 91
Mau-Mau, 51–2
Maughold, 36, 42, 79–81
Maye, Glen, 75 *et seq.*, 104
Mayflower, The, 97
Michael, 68
Milner, 60, 86
Milner's Tower, 86
Milntown, 97
Mint, The, 40
Mona, Glen, 20, 90, 114
Mona's Herald, 30
Mona's Isle, S.S., 31
Mona's Queen, 13, 31
Mona Relief Society, 27
Monks' Bridge, 62, 127
Montacute, Sir William de, 39
Monte, H. de Bello, 40, 62
Moore, George, 76
Moore, Ramsey, 129, 131–2
Moors, The, 36
Moray, Thomas, Earl of, 36
Mourne, Mountains of, 59, 85, 116
Murray, Bishop G., 61
Museums, 25, 31, 49, 83–4, 96, 129, 140, 147
Museum, Castletown Nautical, 123
Museum, Folk, 57
Museum, York Folk, 53
Muster Cross, The, 43

National Trust, The, 20, 57 *et seq.*, 67, 104, 146
Neagh, Lough, 129
Neb Valley, 133
Newcastle-upon-Tyne, 38, 126
Niarbyl, 73, 118
Nicholson, Wm., 131
Nineholes, The, 99
Noble, Henry, 143
North American Manx Association, 27
Norsemen, 64, 82, 130, 151
Nunnery, The, 13, 19, 25, 72, 78, 84, 137–8, 140, 145
Nun's Chairs, The, 117

Ogam, 62
Onchan, 70
Outher, Earl, 133
Orange Day, 89
Orry The Dane, King, 9, 31, 71, 79, 151

Panama Canal, 91
Parishes, Vicar and Captains of, 14–15
Patrick, 75, 132, 133
Peel, 16, 17, 24, 47, 67, 74, 100 *et seq.*, 113, 145, 150
Peel Castle, 43, 44, 46, 97, 102
Peel Cathedral, 102
Peggy, schooner, 123
Pilgrim Fathers, 97
Plains of Heaven, 146
Popplewell, J. A., 58
Port Erin, 33, 58, 85 *et seq.*, 111, 115, 119
Port Jack, 70
Port Moar, 114
Port St. Mary, 17, 24, 53 *et seq.*, 58, 59, 61, 74, 83, 86, 87, 116, 120–1, *et passim*
Port Soderick, 11, 22, 30, 116, 117, 118
Priest's House, 136
Purwick Bay, 55, 121

Quarry Bend, 109
Quarter Bridge, 106, 109
Quayle, Anthony, 92
Quayle, George, 123
Quayle, Capt. Walter, 123
Quayle's Bank, 49
Quilliam, John, 61–2, 125

Raglan, Lord, 38
Ramsey, 21, 30, 47, 64, 70, 90 *et seq.*, 114, 138, *et passim*
Ramsey Bay, 21, 135
Reginald, King of Man, 74
'Rest and Be Thankful' house, 91
Ronaldsway Airport, 38, 45, 88, 95, 122, 124, 126
Round Table, The, 73
Roy, Glen, 69–70
Rushen, 34, 61
Rushen Abbey, 48, 82, 103, 126–7, 138
Rushen, Castle, 34, 38 *et seq.*, 45, 46, 48, 62, 64–5, 80, 127
Rushen, Glen, 75, 76
Rutter, Bishop, 102

St. Bridget, 72, 137–8
St. Catherine's Well, 87
St. Cecilia (St. Kickle), 96
St. German, 76
St. John's, 14, 17, 74, 76, 82, 113, 140
St. John's Hill, 141
St. Mark's, 72
St. Mary, 48, 49
St. Mary Ballure, 81
St. Mary de Douglas, 138
St. Mathew's, 108, 119
St. Olaf, 148
St. Patrick, 18, 76

INDEX

St. Patrick's Chair, 146
St. Patrick's Isle, 102
Santwat, Battle of, 133
Scarlett, 38, 118
Scott, Sir Giles, 92
Seafield, 148
Sheadings, 15
Silverburn, 62, 127
Silverdale, 62–3
Slieuwhallian, 147
Smelt, Cornelius, 50
Snaefell, 22, 65, 69–70, 108, 110, 114, 125
Snaefell, S.S., 31
Sodor and Man, Bishop of, 14, 134
Spanish Head, 57, 121
Spooyt Vane, Glen, 135–6
Standish, Capt. Miles, 97
Stanley family, 41 *et seq.*, 123, 130
Stanley, Sir John, 135
State, Sword of, 36, 130
Stenning, Canon E. H., 112, 125, 127
Stevenson, Sir Ralph, 53
Stowell, Thomas, 69–70
Strews, The, 94
Sugar Loaf Rock, 56
Sulby, 43, 65 *et seq.*, 97, 113
Sulby, River, 93

Taubman, John, 72, 137
Teare, 150
Tholt-y-Will, 68, 69
Thurot, Francois, 135
Tilting Ground, 103
Tower of Refuge, 140

Trollaby, 148
T.T. Races, 13, 22, 69, 82, 107 *et seq.*
Tynwald, 14, 15, 32, 36, 37, 41, 74, 100, 125, 130, 135
Tynwald Day, 27, 37
Tynwald Hill, 14
Tynwald, S.S., 31

Via Regia, 64, 82
Victoria Pier, 98–9
Victoria, Queen, 21, 22, 30
Vikings, 26, 54, 58, 74, 80, 130
Viking, S.S., 32
Villa Marine, 25, 30, 63, 83, 122, 143

Walpole Farm, 66
Ward, Bishop, 64
Welch, John, 140
'West Wood', 75
White, Sir George, V.C., 108
White Lady of Ballafreer, The, 77
Wilks, Sir Mark, 108
Wilson, Bishop, 76, 134
Witch burning, 16
Witches' Kitchen, The, 50
Wren, Hunting of the, 149
Wyllin Glen, 113, 134

Yacht Club, Isle of Man, 55